PERU

TRAVEL GUIDE 2025

Unlocking the Secrets of the Inca Empire: From Machu Picchu to the Amazon Rainforest

Ann W. Smith

Copyright © 2025

All rights reserved. No part of this book may be reproduced, distributed, or transmitted in any form or by any means, including photocopying, recording, or other electronic or mechanical methods, without the prior written permission of the publisher, except in the case of brief quotations embodied in critical reviews and certain other non-commercial uses permitted by copyright law.

DISCLAIMER

The information provided in this travel guide, is intended for general informational purposes only. While every effort has been made to ensure the accuracy and reliability of the content, the author, Sophia J. Regan, and the publisher make no representations or warranties of any kind, express or implied, about the completeness, accuracy, reliability, suitability, or availability of the information contained herein.

Travel conditions, safety guidelines, health recommendations, and other relevant details may change over time. Readers are advised to verify any information and seek professional advice where necessary, especially concerning health, safety, and travel arrangements.

The author and publisher do not assume any responsibility or liability for any loss, damage, or inconvenience caused as a result of reliance on the information provided in this guide. Any reliance placed on such information is strictly at the reader's own risk.

By using this guide, you acknowledge and agree to this disclaimer in full.

ABOUT THE AUTHOR

Ann W. Smith is a passionate traveler, writer, and cultural enthusiast who has explored some of the world's most captivating destinations. With a love for storytelling and a keen eye for detail, she shares her experiences and insights to inspire fellow travelers.

Background and Inspiration

Ann's adventures began at a young age, driven by a fascination with new places and cultures. Peru's rich history, stunning landscapes, and vibrant traditions have particularly captured her heart, fueling her desire to share its wonders with others.

Writing Style

Known for her vivid descriptions and practical advice, Ann combines thorough research with personal anecdotes. Her guides are designed to be both informative and inspiring, helping travelers explore with confidence.

Ann advocates for responsible tourism that respects local cultures and environments. She encourages travelers to make conscious choices that positively impact the places they visit.

ABOUT THE BOOK

This guide is meticulously crafted to provide travelers with in-depth insights, practical tips, and inspiring stories that will help them make the most of their journey through this extraordinary country.

Highlights:

- **Cultural Treasures:** Explore iconic sites like Machu Picchu, the Sacred Valley, and Cusco, delving into the ancient history and traditions of the Inca Empire.
- **Natural Wonders:** Experience the breathtaking beauty of Peru's diverse landscapes, from the Andes mountains to the Amazon rainforest and Lake Titicaca.
- **Culinary Delights:** Discover Peru's world-renowned cuisine with guides to must-try dishes, local beverages, and food tours.
- **Adventure Activities:** Engage in thrilling outdoor sports like trekking, surfing, and wildlife **expeditions.**
- **Practical Information:** Get essential travel tips, safety guidelines, and transportation options to navigate Peru with ease.

Appendix:

- Packing Checklist
- Useful Spanish Phrases
- Emergency Contacts
- Recommended Reading and Viewing
- Local Etiquette and Customs
- Important Websites and Apps

This Travel Guide is designed to enrich your travel experience, providing everything you need to explore Peru confidently and curiously. Whether you're a first-time visitor or a seasoned traveler, this guide ensures an unforgettable adventure.

TABLE OF CONTENTS

Chapter 1: Introduction 9
    Welcome to Peru 11
    Why Visit Peru 14

Chapter 2: Getting There 18
    Major Airports and Airlines 18
    Visa and Entry Requirements 22
    Flights from Major Cities 25

Chapter 3: When to Visit 28
    Seasons and Weather 28
    Packing Tips for Different Seasons 31

Chapter 4: Top Destinations 35
    Machu Picchu 35
    Lima 39
    Cusco 44
    Arequipa 48
    Amazon Rainforest 53

Chapter 5: Accommodation 58
    Luxury Hotels 58
    Mid-Range Hotels 63
    Budget Hostels 68
    Unique Stays 73
    Booking Tips and Recommendations 77

Chapter 6: Food and Drink 83
    Must-Try Dishes 83
    Top Restaurants in Major Cities 88
    Local Beverages 89
    Food Tours and Culinary Experiences 94

Chapter 7: Culture and Customs...........................100
　Basic Language Phrases......................................100
　Etiquette and Social Customs.............................103
　Festivals and Celebrations................................. 107
Chapter 8: Adventure Activities............................ 113
　Hiking Trails... 113
　Wildlife and Nature Tours.................................. 118
　Outdoor Sports... 123
　Adventure Tour Operators................................. 129
Chapter 9: Practical Information............................135
　Currency and Money Exchange.......................... 135
　Safety and Health.. 139
　Transportation...144
　Travel Tips... 150
Chapter 10: Conclusion.. 156
　Summarizing the Journey................................... 156
APPENDIX.. 160
　MAPS...163

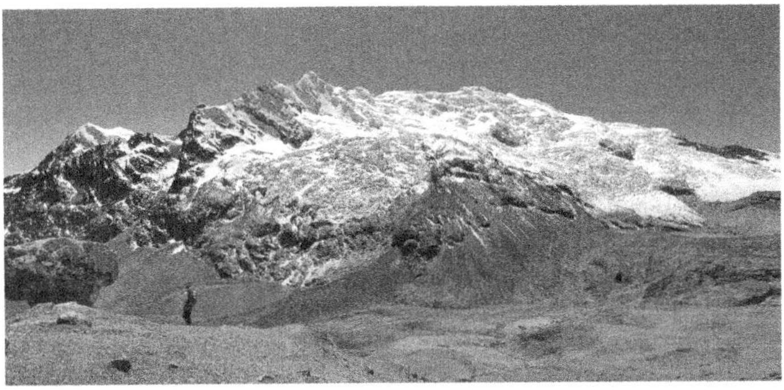

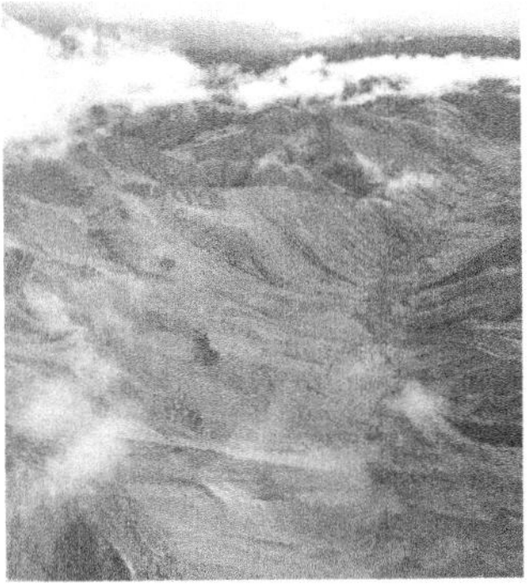

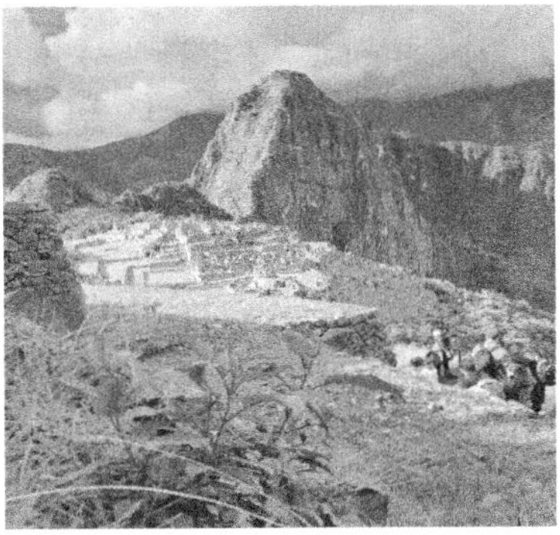

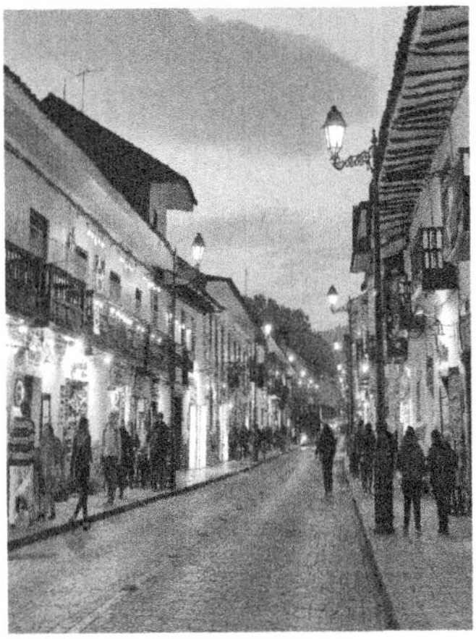

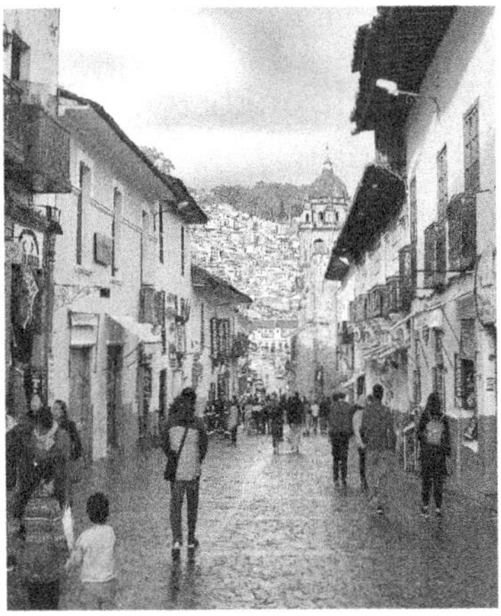

Chapter 1: Introduction

The sun was just beginning to rise over the horizon as my plane descended towards Lima, casting a golden hue across the sprawling city below. I had dreamed of visiting Peru for years, and now, finally, my adventure was about to begin.

From the moment I stepped off the plane, the air felt different—crisp and invigorating, filled with the promise of new experiences. Lima greeted me with a vibrant mix of modernity and history, its streets alive with the sounds of honking taxis, lively street vendors, and the distant hum of the Pacific Ocean. The city's energy was contagious, drawing me into its embrace.

My journey took me from the bustling capital to the ancient heart of the Inca civilization in Cusco. Walking through the cobblestone streets, I felt the weight of history beneath my feet. The colonial architecture whispered tales of a bygone era, while the remnants of Incan temples stood as silent sentinels of a proud and enduring culture.

The highlight of my trip was the awe-inspiring Machu Picchu. As I hiked the Inca Trail, the landscape unfolded like a living tapestry—lush green valleys, towering peaks, and the distant roar of waterfalls. Reaching the Sun Gate at sunrise, I was greeted by the sight of the ancient citadel emerging from the mist, an unforgettable panorama that took my breath away.

The adventure didn't stop there. My travels led me into the heart of the Amazon rainforest, where the dense canopy teemed with life. Monkeys chattered in the trees above, while vibrant butterflies flitted through the air. Guided by a local expert, I learned about the delicate balance of this ecosystem and marveled at the myriad of creatures that called it home.

Of course, no journey to Peru would be complete without indulging in its culinary delights. From the tangy ceviche in coastal Lima to the hearty lomo saltado in the highlands, every meal was a celebration of flavors. And sipping a pisco sour as the sun set over the Andean mountains was the perfect way to end each day.

Peru is a land of contrasts, where ancient traditions blend seamlessly with modern life, and where every corner holds a new discovery. My journey through this captivating country was filled with moments of wonder and awe, leaving me with memories that will last a lifetime.

Welcome to Peru

Imagine stepping into a land where the past and present coexist in vibrant harmony, a place where every corner tells a story. Welcome to Peru, a country that invites you to explore its rich history, breathtaking landscapes, and dynamic culture.

As you arrive in Peru, you'll find yourself in a land of diverse beauty. From the bustling streets of Lima, the coastal capital, to the serene highlands of Cusco, and the verdant expanses of the Amazon Rainforest, Peru's landscapes are as varied as they are stunning. Each region offers its own unique charm and adventures, ensuring that every traveler finds something to captivate their heart.

In Lima, the culinary capital of South America, you'll be greeted with the tantalizing aromas of local cuisine. Whether it's savoring a fresh plate of ceviche by the sea or exploring the city's rich colonial architecture, Lima promises an introduction to Peru's vibrant life. Wander through the historic center, a UNESCO World Heritage site, and marvel at the intricate balconies and majestic plazas that speak of a storied past.

Journeying to Cusco, the ancient heart of the Inca Empire, you'll feel as though you've stepped back in time. The cobblestone streets and historical sites whisper tales of glory and mystique. Here, you can explore the sacred Incan ruins, visit the bustling San Pedro Market, and immerse yourself in the colorful traditions that have been preserved for centuries.

For those seeking nature's wonders, the Amazon Rainforest awaits. This immense and lush jungle, teeming with wildlife, offers an unparalleled experience of biodiversity. Guided by local experts, you can navigate the winding rivers, observe exotic creatures in their natural habitat, and learn about the delicate balance of this precious ecosystem.

No visit to Peru is complete without witnessing the awe-inspiring beauty of Machu Picchu. As the sun rises over the Andean peaks, revealing the ancient citadel shrouded in mist, you'll understand why this site is one of the New Seven Wonders of the World. The journey to Machu Picchu, whether by the famous Inca Trail or a scenic train ride, is as memorable as the destination itself.

Beyond its natural and historical treasures, Peru is a country of warmth and hospitality. The Peruvian people, with their diverse cultural heritage, are known for their friendliness and welcoming spirit. Engaging with locals, you'll discover a tapestry of languages, traditions, and celebrations that reflect the rich mosaic of Peru's identity.

So, welcome to Peru—a place where every adventure is a discovery, every encounter a story. Whether you're exploring ancient ruins, trekking through stunning landscapes, or simply savoring the flavors of Peruvian cuisine, your journey here promises to be unforgettable.

Why Visit Peru

As I stood on the edge of the Sun Gate, looking out over the mist-shrouded ruins of Machu Picchu, I knew why visiting Peru was more than just a trip—it was a journey through time and culture, a chance to experience the world's wonders firsthand.

Peru offers a unique blend of natural beauty, rich history, and vibrant culture that appeals to every type of traveler. Here are some compelling reasons to visit this captivating country:

1. Ancient History and Archaeological Wonders
   - **Machu Picchu:** This iconic Incan citadel is one of the New Seven Wonders of the World. Walking

through its ancient stone paths, you can almost hear the whispers of the past.

   - **Sacred Valley and Cusco:** Once the heart of the Inca Empire, Cusco and the Sacred Valley are dotted with impressive ruins, temples, and terraced landscapes, each with stories waiting to be discovered.

   - **Nazca Lines:** These mysterious geoglyphs etched into the desert floor are still a subject of wonder and speculation. Seen best from the air, they depict animals, plants, and geometric shapes.

2. Stunning Natural Landscapes

   - **The Andes Mountains:** Towering peaks and serene valleys provide perfect backdrops for hiking and exploring. The Inca Trail offers one of the most scenic treks in the world, leading you through diverse terrains to the gates of Machu Picchu.

   - **Amazon Rainforest:** The Peruvian Amazon is one of the most biodiverse places on Earth. You can embark on guided tours to explore its rich flora and fauna, spotting exotic wildlife like jaguars, pink dolphins, and countless bird species.

   - **Lake Titicaca:** The highest navigable lake in the world, straddling the border between Peru and Bolivia. It's home to the unique Uros floating islands, made entirely of reeds.

3. Culinary Delights

- **Gastronomy:** Peru is a food lover's paradise, renowned for its innovative cuisine that blends indigenous ingredients with global influences. From the fresh tang of ceviche to the hearty flavors of lomo saltado, every meal is an adventure.

- **Street Food:** Don't miss trying street snacks like anticuchos (grilled beef heart skewers) and picarones (sweet potato doughnuts) while exploring local markets.

4. Cultural Richness and Festivals

- **Diverse Cultures**: Peru is a melting pot of cultures, where indigenous traditions blend with Spanish, African, and Asian influences. This is reflected in everything from music and dance to art and festivals.

- **Festivals**: Throughout the year, Peru hosts vibrant festivals that celebrate its rich heritage. Inti Raymi, the Festival of the Sun, is a spectacular re-enactment of Incan ceremonies held in Cusco. The colorful Puno Week celebrates the founding of the city with parades, music, and traditional dances.

5. Warm and Welcoming People

- **Hospitality**: The Peruvian people are known for their warmth and friendliness. Engaging with locals, whether in bustling cities or remote villages, provides a deeper understanding of the country's soul.

6. Adventure and Exploration

- **Outdoor Activities:** Whether you're hiking the rugged trails of the Andes, sandboarding in the coastal desert of Huacachina, or surfing the waves in Mancora, Peru offers a plethora of adventurous activities.

- **Ecotourism**: Sustainable tourism initiatives allow you to experience Peru's natural beauty while supporting local communities and conservation efforts.

Peru is a destination that promises to awaken your sense of wonder and adventure. Each region offers its own unique experiences, ensuring that every traveler finds something extraordinary. From the heights of the Andes to the depths of the Amazon, Peru is a country that captivates the heart and soul, leaving you with memories that last a lifetime.

Chapter 2: Getting There

Major Airports and Airlines

When planning your trip to Peru, knowing the major airports and airlines can help ensure a smooth start to your adventure. Here's a guide to the key entry points and the airlines that can get you there.

➤ **Major Airports**

1. Jorge Chávez International Airport (LIM) – Lima

   - Location: Situated in Callao, about 10 kilometers northwest of Lima's city center.
   - Overview: This is the primary international and domestic airport in Peru, handling the majority of the country's air traffic. It offers a wide range of amenities, including restaurants, shops, and car rental services.
   - Facilities: Free Wi-Fi, VIP lounges, duty-free shops, and currency exchange services.

- Transportation: Taxis, shuttle services, and public buses connect the airport to various parts of Lima.

2. Alejandro Velasco Astete International Airport (CUZ) – Cusco

- Location: Located about 3 miles southeast of the historic city center of Cusco.
- Overview: This airport is the gateway to the Sacred Valley and Machu Picchu. While smaller than Lima's airport, it still handles a significant amount of traffic, particularly tourists heading to the Incan sites.
- Facilities: Cafes, souvenir shops, and car rental services.
- Transportation: Taxis and shuttle services are available to take you to the city center and nearby hotels.

3. Rodríguez Ballón International Airport (AQP) – Arequipa

- Location: Positioned 8 kilometers northwest of Arequipa's city center.
- Overview: This airport serves the southern region of Peru and is an important hub for travelers visiting the Colca Canyon and surrounding areas.
- Facilities: Restaurants, shops, and basic amenities.

- Transportation: Taxis and buses provide connections to the city and surrounding areas.

4. Coronel FAP Francisco Secada Vignetta International Airport (IQT) – Iquitos
   - Location: About 7 kilometers southeast of downtown Iquitos.
   - Overview: This airport is the main gateway to the Peruvian Amazon. It primarily handles domestic flights, but also has some international connections.
   - Facilities: Basic amenities including cafes and shops.
   - Transportation: Taxis and mototaxis (three-wheeled vehicles) are common for transportation into the city.

➢ **Major Airlines**

1. LATAM Airlines
   - Overview: As the largest airline in Latin America, LATAM offers extensive domestic and international flight options. It is known for its reliability and comprehensive network.
   - Destinations: Major cities in North America, Europe, Asia, and across South America.

2. Avianca

- Overview: A leading airline in South America, Avianca provides a robust network of flights throughout the region.
   - Destinations: Primarily focuses on routes within South America, Central America, and select destinations in North America and Europe.

3. Sky Airline
   - Overview: A low-cost carrier based in Chile, Sky Airline offers affordable flights within Peru and to neighboring countries.
   - Destinations: Domestic routes within Peru and international flights to Chile and other nearby countries.

4. Viva Air Peru
   - Overview: Another budget-friendly airline, Viva Air Peru offers numerous domestic flights, making it a convenient option for traveling within the country.
   - Destinations: Primarily domestic flights connecting major cities within Peru.

5. Star Peru
   - Overview: A regional airline that provides domestic flights to several destinations across Peru.
   - Destinations: Focuses on smaller cities and regions, including popular tourist destinations.

Visa and Entry Requirements

When planning your trip to Peru, it's important to understand the visa and entry requirements to ensure a smooth arrival. Here's what you need to know:

> ➢ **Visa Requirements**

1. Tourist Visa:
   - Who Needs It: Citizens of most countries need a tourist visa to visit Peru. However, nationals from countries like the United States, Canada, the United Kingdom, Australia, and many others do not need a visa for tourism purposes.
   - Application: If you need a visa, you must apply at the Peruvian consulate or embassy in your home country. The application should be submitted at least 15 days before your trip.
   - Duration: The tourist visa allows you to stay in Peru for up to 90 days. This period cannot be extended.

2. Business Visa:
   - Who Needs It: If you plan to visit Peru for business purposes, you will need a business visa.

This applies even to citizens from countries that do not require a tourist visa.

- Application: Similar to the tourist visa, you must apply for a business visa at the Peruvian consulate or embassy in your home country.

3. Other Visas:

- Longer Stays: For stays longer than 90 days, or for purposes other than tourism or business (such as studying or working), you will need to apply for the relevant visa.

- Extensions: If you need to extend your stay, you must apply for an extension with the National Superintendence of Migration in Peru before your initial visa expires.

➢ **Entry Requirements**

1. Passport:

- Validity: Your passport must be valid for at least six months from the date of entry into Peru.

- Condition: Ensure your passport has at least two blank pages for entry and exit stamps.

2. Travel Itinerary:

- Proof of Departure: You may be required to show proof of your onward travel or return ticket.

3. Accommodation Details:
    - Where You'll Stay: Be prepared to provide information about your accommodation in Peru.

4. Health Insurance:
    - Coverage: It's recommended to have travel health insurance that covers medical emergencies.

5. Customs Declaration:
    - Baggage: When entering Peru, you must correctly complete a baggage declaration form if you have items to declare.

   ➢ **Additional Tips**

- Contact Local Authorities: Entry and exit conditions can change at short notice, so it's a good idea to contact the nearest Peruvian embassy or consulate for the latest information.
- Visa-Free Entry: Citizens of certain countries, including many in Latin America and Europe, can enter Peru without a visa for tourism purposes.

By following these guidelines, you can ensure a hassle-free entry into Peru and enjoy your travels with peace of mind.

Flights from Major Cities

Traveling to Peru from major cities around the world is quite accessible, thanks to numerous direct and connecting flights. Here's a guide to help you plan your journey:

From the United States
- Direct Flights: Major cities like Miami, New York, Fort Lauderdale, Orlando, Atlanta, and Dallas offer nonstop flights to Lima.
- Connecting Flights: Other cities can connect through major hubs such as Los Angeles, Houston, or Miami.

From Europe
- Direct Flights: Cities like Amsterdam, Frankfurt, Zurich, and Madrid have direct flights to Lima.
- Connecting Flights: Other European cities often connect through these hubs or via other major European airports.

From Asia
- Direct Flights: Tokyo, Seoul, and Dubai offer direct flights to Lima.

- Connecting Flights: Other Asian cities typically connect through these hubs or via other major Asian airports.

From South America
- Direct Flights: Cities like Santiago (Chile), Bogotá (Colombia), and Buenos Aires (Argentina) have direct flights to Lima.
- Connecting Flights: Other South American cities often connect through these hubs.

From Oceania
- Direct Flights: Sydney and Auckland offer direct flights to Lima.
- Connecting Flights: Other cities in Oceania typically connect through these hubs or via other major airports.

From Africa
- Direct Flights: Johannesburg offers direct flights to Lima.
- Connecting Flights: Other African cities often connect through Johannesburg or other major international hubs.

From Canada
- Direct Flights: Toronto and Vancouver offer direct flights to Lima.

- Connecting Flights: Other Canadian cities typically connect through these hubs or via other major international airports.

By choosing the right departure city and airline, you can find convenient and comfortable flights to Peru. Make sure to book your tickets in advance to get the best deals and ensure a smooth travel experience.

Chapter 3: When to Visit

Seasons and Weather

Peru is a country of diverse climates and landscapes, which means the best time to visit can vary depending on where you're headed and what you're looking to do. Here's a breakdown of the seasons and weather to help you plan your trip:

Coastal Region (Lima and Northern Beaches)
- Summer (December to March): This is the best time to visit the coast, with warm temperatures and plenty of sunshine. Lima sees less fog and more sunny days, making it ideal for exploring the city and enjoying the beaches.
- Winter (June to September): During these months, the coast experiences cooler temperatures and foggy conditions, particularly in Lima. However, northern beaches like Mancora remain warm and sunny, perfect for beach lovers.

Andean Highlands (Cusco, Machu Picchu, and Lake Titicaca)
- Dry Season (May to September): This is the peak tourist season in the highlands, with clear skies and minimal rainfall. It's the best time for trekking, including the Inca Trail to Machu Picchu. Nights can be chilly, so pack layers.
- Wet Season (November to March): During this period, the highlands experience frequent rain showers, which can make hiking trails muddy and challenging. However, the landscapes are lush and green, and there are fewer tourists. Machu Picchu remains open year-round.

Amazon Rainforest (Iquitos and Puerto Maldonado)
- Dry Season (April to November): This is the preferred time to visit the Amazon, with lower water levels making it easier to explore the jungle and spot wildlife. The weather is still hot and humid, but there are fewer mosquitoes.
- Wet Season (December to March): The Amazon receives heavy rainfall during these months, which can lead to flooding. However, it's an excellent time for boat tours as the water levels are higher. Expect hot and humid conditions, with plenty of rain.

❖ Seasons at a Glance

- **High Season (May to September):**
  - Ideal for trekking and exploring the Andean highlands.
  - Clear skies, dry weather, but higher tourist crowds.
  - Key months: June (Inti Raymi festival in Cusco), July and August (busiest months).

- **Shoulder Season (April and October):**
  - A great time for fewer crowds and good weather in both the highlands and the coast.
  - Ideal for travelers looking to balance good weather with fewer tourists.

- **Low Season (November to March):**
  - Best for visiting the coastal region for beach activities.
  - Rainy season in the highlands and Amazon, but lush landscapes and fewer tourists.
  - Key month: December (Christmas celebrations).

❖ **Packing Tips**

- Coastal Region: Light, breathable clothing for summer; layers for cooler, foggy winter days.
- Andean Highlands: Layers, including warm clothes for cold nights; waterproof gear for the wet season.

- Amazon Rainforest: Lightweight, breathable clothing; long sleeves and pants to protect against insects; waterproof gear.

Peru's varied climates ensure there's something to enjoy year-round. By understanding the seasonal differences, you can choose the best time to visit based on your interests and desired activities.

Packing Tips for Different Seasons

Packing for a trip to Peru can be quite the adventure itself, given the country's diverse climates and landscapes. Whether you're headed to the coastal regions, the Andean highlands, or the Amazon rainforest, here are some essential packing tips tailored for different seasons:

Coastal Region (Lima and Northern Beaches)

Summer (December to March):
- Light Clothing: Pack breathable, lightweight fabrics like cotton or linen to stay cool in the summer heat.
- Swimwear: Don't forget your swimsuit, as you'll want to take advantage of the beautiful beaches.

- Sun Protection: Bring sunscreen, sunglasses, and a wide-brimmed hat to protect against the strong coastal sun.
- Light Jacket: Evenings can sometimes be cooler, so a light jacket or sweater is handy.

Winter (June to September):
- Layers: The coastal region can be cooler and foggy during winter, so pack layers such as long-sleeve shirts and sweaters.
- Warm Jacket: A warm jacket is essential for chilly mornings and evenings.
- Comfortable Shoes: Pack comfortable walking shoes for exploring Lima's historical sites and neighborhoods.

Andean Highlands (Cusco, Machu Picchu, and Lake Titicaca)

Dry Season (May to September):
- Layered Clothing: The weather can change quickly in the highlands, so pack layers. Include t-shirts, long-sleeve shirts, and a warm fleece or jacket.
- Warm Accessories: Gloves, a hat, and a scarf are essential for cold mornings and nights.
- Sturdy Hiking Boots: Good quality, waterproof hiking boots are a must if you plan to trek the Inca Trail or other paths.

- Sun Protection: High altitudes mean stronger UV rays, so bring sunscreen, sunglasses, and a hat.

Wet Season (November to March):
- Waterproof Gear: A waterproof jacket and pants will keep you dry during frequent rain showers.
- Quick-Dry Clothing: Pack clothing made of quick-dry materials to stay comfortable.
- Rain Poncho: A lightweight rain poncho is useful for sudden downpours.
- Warm Layers: Despite the rain, temperatures can still drop, so bring warm layers and accessories.

Amazon Rainforest (Iquitos and Puerto Maldonado)

Dry Season (April to November):
- Light, Breathable Clothing: Long-sleeve shirts and long pants made of lightweight, breathable fabric will protect against insects and the heat.
- Insect Repellent: Essential for keeping mosquitoes at bay.
- Sun Protection: Sunscreen, sunglasses, and a wide-brimmed hat for protection against the sun.
- Sturdy Shoes: Waterproof hiking boots or sturdy shoes for jungle treks.
- Waterproof Bags: Protect your belongings from humidity and occasional rain.

Wet Season (December to March):
- Waterproof Gear: A waterproof jacket and pants are necessary for heavy rain.
- Light Layers: Even in the wet season, it remains hot and humid, so pack light, breathable layers.
- Waterproof Footwear: Rubber boots or waterproof shoes are ideal for walking through wet terrain.
- Mosquito Net: A portable mosquito net can be useful for sleeping, even in lodges.

General Packing Tips
- Reusable Water Bottle: Stay hydrated, especially in high altitudes and hot climates.
- First Aid Kit: Include basic medical supplies, any prescription medications, and remedies for common ailments like altitude sickness.
- Backpack or Daypack: A small, comfortable backpack for day trips and hikes.
- Travel Adapters: Check the electrical outlet types and bring the necessary travel adapters.
- Personal Hygiene Items: Travel-sized toiletries, hand sanitizer, and wet wipes.

By packing smartly and considering the season and region you're visiting, you'll be prepared for anything Peru has to offer

Chapter 4: Top Destinations

Machu Picchu

Nestled high in the Andes Mountains, Machu Picchu is one of the most iconic and awe-inspiring destinations in the world. This ancient Incan city, often referred to as the "Lost City of the Incas," offers a glimpse into a fascinating civilization and provides an unforgettable experience for travelers.

- ### History and Significance

Machu Picchu was built in the 15th century under the reign of Inca Emperor Pachacuti. It served as an estate for the emperor and a sacred religious site. Despite its prominence, the city was abandoned during the Spanish conquest and remained hidden from the outside world until its rediscovery in 1911 by American explorer Hiram Bingham.

The site is now a UNESCO World Heritage site and one of the New Seven Wonders of the World, attracting visitors from across the globe who come to marvel at its architectural ingenuity and natural beauty.

- ### How to Get There

Reaching Machu Picchu can be an adventure in itself, with several routes available:

1. *Inca Trail:*
 - Overview: The Inca Trail is the most famous trekking route to Machu Picchu, offering stunning scenery and a sense of accomplishment.
 - Duration: The classic trek takes about 4 days and 3 nights, though shorter options are available.
 - Permits: A limited number of permits are issued each day, so booking well in advance is essential.

2. *Train:*
 - Overview: For those who prefer a more relaxed journey, trains run from Cusco and the Sacred Valley to Aguas Calientes, the town at the base of Machu Picchu.
 - Operators: The two main train operators are PeruRail and Inca Rail, offering various classes of service.

- Duration: The train journey takes about 3.5 to 4 hours from Cusco.

3. Bus and Walking:
- From Aguas Calientes: A bus service operates from Aguas Calientes to the entrance of Machu Picchu. Alternatively, you can hike up the steep path, which takes about 1 to 1.5 hours.

- What to See

Machu Picchu is divided into two main areas: the agricultural sector, with its famous terraces, and the urban sector, where you'll find temples, plazas, and residential areas. Key highlights include:

1. Intihuatana Stone: A ritual stone associated with astronomy and the solstices, considered one of the most important features of Machu Picchu.

2. Temple of the Sun: An impressive structure dedicated to Inti, the Incan sun god, with intricate stonework and a commanding view of the surrounding area.

3. Room of the Three Windows: Named for its three trapezoidal windows, this structure offers a stunning view of the Sacred Plaza.

4. The Main Plaza: The central area of the city, where important ceremonies and gatherings took place.

5. The Guardhouse: Located at the top of the terraces, offering panoramic views of the entire site and the surrounding mountains.

- Tips for Visiting

1. Book in Advance: Entrance tickets to Machu Picchu are limited and must be purchased in advance. This is especially important for the Inca Trail and Huayna Picchu hike permits.
2. Early Morning Visit: Arriving early allows you to experience the site with fewer crowds and catch the sunrise over the mountains.
3. Guided Tours: Consider hiring a local guide to gain deeper insights into the history and significance of Machu Picchu.
4. Weather Preparation: The weather can change quickly, so bring layers, a rain jacket, and sun protection.
5. Respect the Site: Machu Picchu is a fragile archaeological site, so follow all guidelines to help preserve its beauty for future generations.

Visiting Machu Picchu is a journey back in time, offering a unique opportunity to connect with the ancient Incan civilization and witness one of the world's most stunning historical landmarks.

Lima

Lima, the vibrant capital of Peru, is a bustling metropolis that seamlessly blends modernity with history. Overlooking the Pacific Ocean, this coastal city is known for its rich cultural heritage, dynamic arts scene, and, most notably, its world-renowned cuisine. Here's a closer look at what makes Lima a must-visit destination.

- Top Attractions

1. Historic Center of Lima:
   - Plaza Mayor: The heart of the city, surrounded by historical buildings such as the Government Palace, the Cathedral of Lima, and the Archbishop's Palace.
   - San Francisco Monastery: Famous for its stunning architecture and catacombs, which house the remains of thousands of people from colonial times.

2. Miraflores:

- Larcomar: A shopping and entertainment complex perched on cliffs overlooking the ocean, offering stunning views and a variety of restaurants and shops.

- Huaca Pucllana: An ancient adobe and clay pyramid dating back to the Lima culture, located right in the middle of the modern city.

- Parque Kennedy: A vibrant park often bustling with activities, local art, and the famous "cat park" where friendly felines roam.

3. Barranco:

- Bridge of Sighs (Puente de los Suspiros): A charming wooden bridge that is a favorite spot for couples and local legends.

- Street Art and Murals: This bohemian district is known for its colorful street art and murals that tell the story of the city's cultural evolution.

- Bajada de los Baños: A scenic path leading from the district down to the coast, lined with cafes, bars, and art galleries.

- Culinary Delights

Lima has earned its title as the culinary capital of South America, thanks to its innovative chefs and rich culinary traditions. Here are some must-try dishes and dining experiences:

1. Ceviche: The national dish of Peru, made from fresh fish marinated in lime juice, onions, cilantro, and aji peppers. It's often served with corn and sweet potatoes.

2. Lomo Saltado: A flavorful stir-fry that combines marinated beef with onions, tomatoes, and potatoes, typically served with rice.

3. Anticuchos: Skewers of marinated beef heart, grilled to perfection and often served with potatoes and a spicy aji sauce.

4. Pisco Sour: Peru's iconic cocktail, made with pisco (a type of brandy), lime juice, simple syrup, egg white, and bitters.

- Top Restaurants

- **Central**: Ranked among the best restaurants in the world, Central offers a tasting menu that explores Peru's diverse ecosystems and ingredients.
- **Maido**: Renowned for its unique blend of Peruvian and Japanese flavors, a cuisine known as Nikkei.
- **Astrid y Gastón**: A flagship restaurant of famed chef Gastón Acurio, offering a modern take on traditional Peruvian dishes.

- **La Mar**: A cevicheria where you can enjoy some of the freshest and most delicious ceviche in the city.

- Cultural Experiences

1. Museo Larco: This museum houses an extensive collection of pre-Columbian art and artifacts, including the famous erotic pottery gallery.
2. Teatro Municipal de Lima: A beautifully restored theater that hosts a variety of performances, from classical music to contemporary dance.
3. Magic Water Circuit (Circuito Mágico del Agua): An enchanting park featuring 13 illuminated fountains that perform choreographed light and water shows in the evening.

- Practical Information

- **Transportation**: Lima has a range of transportation options, including taxis, buses, and the Metropolitano bus rapid transit system. Ride-hailing apps like Uber are also widely available.
- **Accommodation**: From luxury hotels in Miraflores to charming boutique inns in Barranco,

Lima offers a variety of accommodations to suit every budget and taste.

- **Safety Tips:** While Lima is generally safe for tourists, it's advisable to take standard precautions, such as avoiding poorly lit areas at night and being aware of your surroundings.

Lima's mix of historic charm and contemporary flair makes it a captivating destination for any traveler. Whether you're exploring its ancient ruins, indulging in its culinary delights, or soaking up its vibrant culture, Lima promises an unforgettable experience.

Cusco

Cusco, often spelled as Cuzco, is a city steeped in history and culture. Once the capital of the Inca Empire, Cusco is now a bustling hub that attracts travelers from around the world who come to explore its archaeological wonders, vibrant markets, and rich traditions. Nestled in the Andean highlands, this UNESCO World Heritage site serves as the gateway to Machu Picchu and the Sacred Valley.

- Top Attractions

1. Plaza de Armas:
   - Overview: The central square of Cusco, surrounded by colonial arcades, impressive churches, and lively cafes. It's a great place to start your exploration and soak up the local atmosphere.

- Highlights: The Cathedral of Santo Domingo and the Church of the Society of Jesus (Iglesia de la Compañía de Jesús) are architectural masterpieces that dominate the plaza.

2. Qorikancha (Temple of the Sun):
- History: Once the most important temple in the Inca Empire, dedicated to the sun god Inti. The Spanish built the Santo Domingo Convent on its foundations, creating a fascinating blend of Incan and colonial architecture.
- Highlights: The original Inca stonework is still visible, showcasing the advanced engineering skills of the Incas.

3. Sacsayhuamán:
- Overview: An impressive Inca fortress located on a hill overlooking Cusco. Known for its massive stone walls, some of which weigh over 100 tons.
- Activities: Explore the extensive ruins, enjoy panoramic views of the city, and learn about the historical significance of this site.

4. San Pedro Market:
- Overview: A bustling market where locals shop for fresh produce, meats, and everyday goods.

- Highlights: Sample local delicacies, buy colorful textiles, and experience the vibrant energy of Cusco's daily life.

5. The Sacred Valley:
   - Overview: A fertile valley that was crucial to the Incas for agriculture and as a transportation route. It's dotted with Inca ruins, traditional villages, and stunning landscapes.
   - Must-Visit Sites: Pisac (known for its ruins and market), Ollantaytambo (a well-preserved Inca town and fortress), and Chinchero (famous for its textiles and agricultural terraces).

- Cultural Experiences

1. Inti Raymi (Festival of the Sun):
   - Overview: Held every June 24th, this is one of the most important Incan festivals, celebrating the winter solstice and honoring the sun god Inti.
   - Highlights: Re-enactments of Incan ceremonies, processions, and traditional music and dance.

2. Textile Workshops:
   - Activities: Visit local workshops where you can see artisans at work, learn about traditional weaving techniques, and purchase beautiful handwoven textiles.

- Locations: Chinchero and Awana Kancha are popular spots for learning about textile traditions.

3. Culinary Delights:
   - Local Cuisine: Cusco offers a variety of traditional Peruvian dishes, such as cuy (guinea pig), alpaca, and hearty soups like chupe de camarones.
   - Cooking Classes: Join a cooking class to learn how to prepare Peruvian dishes using local ingredients.

- Practical Information

- **Altitude**: Cusco is located at an altitude of 3,400 meters (11,200 feet). To avoid altitude sickness, take it easy on your first day, stay hydrated, and consider drinking coca tea.
- **Getting Around:** The city center is best explored on foot, but taxis and buses are available for longer distances.
- **Accommodation**: From luxury hotels to budget hostels, Cusco offers a range of accommodation options to suit every traveler's needs.
- **Safety Tips:** While Cusco is generally safe for tourists, it's advisable to be cautious with your belongings and avoid walking alone at night in poorly lit areas.

Cusco is a city where history comes alive, offering a unique blend of ancient Incan heritage and vibrant modern culture. Whether you're exploring its impressive ruins, engaging with its local traditions, or simply soaking in the breathtaking views of the Andean landscape, Cusco promises an unforgettable experience.

Arequipa

Nestled at the foot of three towering volcanoes, Arequipa is Peru's second-largest city and a gem of the country's southern region. Known as the "White City" due to its stunning colonial architecture built from white volcanic stone, Arequipa offers a captivating blend of history, culture, and natural beauty.

- Top Attractions

1. Plaza de Armas:

- Overview: The heart of Arequipa, this bustling square is surrounded by impressive colonial buildings, including the Cathedral of Arequipa.

- Highlights: The square is a great place to start your exploration, offering stunning views of the surrounding architecture and the distant volcanoes.

2. Santa Catalina Monastery:

- History: Founded in 1579, this vast convent is a city within a city, with its maze-like streets, colorful walls, and tranquil courtyards.

- Highlights: Visitors can wander through the convent's cloisters, chapels, and living quarters, gaining a glimpse into the lives of the nuns who lived there.

3. Yanahuara District:

- Overview: Known for its narrow streets and traditional homes, this picturesque neighborhood offers some of the best views of the city and the surrounding volcanoes.

- Highlights: The Yanahuara viewpoint provides a panoramic vista of Arequipa, with the majestic El Misti volcano as a backdrop.

4. Colca Canyon:

- Overview: One of the deepest canyons in the world, Colca Canyon is a natural wonder located a few hours from Arequipa. It's twice as deep as the Grand Canyon and offers breathtaking landscapes.

- Activities: Hiking, bird watching (look out for the Andean condor), and visiting traditional villages along the canyon.

5. San Camilo Market:

- Overview: A bustling market where you can experience the vibrant local culture and cuisine.

- Highlights: Sample fresh produce, local cheeses, and traditional dishes. It's a great place to buy souvenirs and immerse yourself in daily life.

- Cultural Experiences

1. Museo Santuarios Andinos:

- Overview: This museum is home to "Juanita," the Inca Ice Maiden, a well-preserved mummy discovered on Mount Ampato.

- Highlights: Learn about Incan rituals and the archaeological significance of this remarkable find.

2. Arequipa's Colonial Architecture:

- Walking Tours: Explore the city's beautifully preserved colonial buildings made from sillar, a white volcanic stone.

- Highlights: The Cathedral of Arequipa, the Church of La Compañía, and various colonial-era mansions like Casa del Moral and Casa de la Moneda.

3. Festivals and Traditions:
- Virgin of Chapi: Celebrated in May, this religious festival attracts thousands of pilgrims to the Sanctuary of Chapi, located in the nearby desert.
- Carnival: Held in February or March, Arequipa's Carnival features vibrant parades, traditional dances, and lively celebrations.

- **Culinary Delights**

1. Traditional Dishes:
- Rocoto Relleno: Spicy stuffed peppers filled with minced meat, vegetables, and cheese.
- Adobo: A hearty pork stew marinated in chicha de jora (corn beer) and spices.
- Chupe de Camarones: A rich shrimp soup, often served with rice, potatoes, and corn.

2. Picanterías:
- Overview: Traditional eateries where you can enjoy Arequipa's unique cuisine in a convivial atmosphere.
- Popular Spots: La Nueva Palomino and La Lucila are renowned for their authentic local dishes.

- **Practical Information**

- Transportation: Arequipa's city center is best explored on foot. For longer distances, taxis and local buses are readily available.
- Accommodation: The city offers a wide range of accommodations, from luxury hotels to budget hostels, many housed in beautiful colonial buildings.
- Safety Tips: Arequipa is generally safe for tourists, but as with any city, it's advisable to stay aware of your surroundings and secure your belongings.

Arequipa's blend of natural beauty, historical richness, and vibrant culture makes it a standout destination in Peru. Whether you're exploring its dramatic landscapes, savoring its culinary specialties, or delving into its fascinating history, Arequipa promises an unforgettable experience.

Amazon Rainforest

The Amazon Rainforest, often referred to as the "lungs of the Earth," is a vast and vibrant ecosystem that spans across several countries in South America, with a significant portion located in Peru. This lush, biodiverse paradise is home to an incredible variety of wildlife, plants, and indigenous cultures, making it a must-visit destination for nature lovers and adventurers alike.

Overview

Peru's Amazon Rainforest is divided into two main regions: the northern Amazon around Iquitos and the southern Amazon near Puerto Maldonado. Each region offers unique experiences and opportunities to explore the dense jungle, teeming with life.

- Top Attractions

1. Manu National Park:

- Overview: A UNESCO World Heritage site, Manu National Park is one of the most biodiverse areas in the world. It covers a range of ecosystems from lowland rainforest to Andean highlands.

- Highlights: Spotting jaguars, giant otters, and over a thousand bird species. The park also offers opportunities to learn about indigenous cultures and their sustainable ways of living.

2. Tambopata National Reserve:

- Location: Located near Puerto Maldonado, this reserve is renowned for its rich biodiversity.

- Highlights: The reserve is home to numerous species of birds, mammals, reptiles, and insects. Visitors can also see macaw clay licks, where hundreds of macaws gather to feed on the mineral-rich clay.

3. Pacaya-Samiria National Reserve:

- Overview: One of the largest protected areas in Peru, located in the northern Amazon near Iquitos.

- Highlights: The reserve offers river cruises where you can spot pink river dolphins, caimans, and a variety of bird species. It's a prime location for experiencing the Amazon's unique flora and fauna.

- Cultural Experiences

1. Indigenous Communities:
   - Visits: Many tours offer the chance to visit indigenous communities, where you can learn about traditional ways of life, crafts, and the use of medicinal plants.
   - Interaction: Engage with local guides who provide insights into the symbiotic relationship between the people and the rainforest.

2. Sustainable Tourism:
   - Eco-Lodges: Stay in eco-friendly lodges that promote sustainable practices and conservation efforts. These lodges often employ locals and contribute to preserving the environment.
   - Education: Many lodges and tour operators provide educational programs about the importance of rainforest conservation and sustainable living.

- Adventure Activities

1. Jungle Treks:
   - Guided Hikes: Explore the rainforest on foot with experienced guides who can point out hidden wildlife, medicinal plants, and explain the complexities of the ecosystem.

- Night Walks: Discover the nocturnal side of the Amazon, where you can spot creatures like tarantulas, frogs, and night monkeys.

2. River Expeditions:
   - Boat Tours: Navigate the winding rivers and tributaries, offering a unique perspective of the Amazon. Look out for caimans, turtles, and the famous pink river dolphins.
   - Canoeing and Kayaking: For a more immersive experience, paddle through smaller waterways and get closer to the natural surroundings.

3. Bird Watching:
   - Diverse Avifauna: The Amazon is a birdwatcher's paradise, with species ranging from colorful macaws to elusive harpy eagles. Guided birdwatching tours can help you spot rare and exotic birds.

- Practical Information

- **Best Time to Visit**: The dry season (June to November) is the best time for wildlife viewing and hiking, with fewer mosquitoes and more navigable trails. The wet season (December to May) offers lush landscapes and higher water levels, ideal for boat tours.

- **Packing Essentials**: Lightweight, breathable clothing, long sleeves and pants for insect protection, waterproof gear, binoculars, and plenty of insect repellent.
- **Health Precautions**: Ensure you have the necessary vaccinations, such as yellow fever, and consider taking anti-malarial medication. Always use mosquito nets and repellent to protect against bites.

The Peruvian Amazon Rainforest is a place of unparalleled natural beauty and biodiversity. Whether you're trekking through dense jungle, cruising along the mighty rivers, or engaging with local communities, the Amazon offers a profound connection to nature and a glimpse into one of the world's most vital ecosystems. An adventure here promises to be as thrilling as it is enlightening.

Chapter 5: Accommodation

Luxury Hotels

Peru offers a range of luxury hotels that combine world-class amenities with unique cultural and natural experiences. Here are some of the top luxury accommodations in key destinations across the country:

★ Lima

1. Belmond Miraflores Park:
   - Overview: Located in the upscale district of Miraflores, this hotel offers stunning ocean views, elegant suites, and exceptional service.
      - Amenities: Rooftop pool, spa, gourmet restaurant, and personalized concierge services.

- Highlight: The rooftop pool area offers breathtaking views of the Pacific Ocean and is perfect for unwinding after a day of exploration.

2. Hotel B:
   - Overview: A boutique luxury hotel in the bohemian Barranco district, housed in a restored Belle Époque mansion.
   - Amenities: Art-filled interiors, fine dining, a cozy bar, and personalized service.
   - Highlight: The hotel's unique blend of contemporary art and historic charm creates an inviting and sophisticated atmosphere.

★ Cusco

1. Belmond Hotel Monasterio:
   - Overview: Housed in a former monastery dating back to 1592, this hotel combines colonial charm with modern luxury.
   - Amenities: Beautiful courtyards, gourmet dining, spa services, and historic architecture.
   - Highlight: The stunning central courtyard and the serene atmosphere make it a perfect retreat in the heart of Cusco.

2. Palacio del Inka, a Luxury Collection Hotel:

- Overview: Situated in a historic mansion, this hotel offers a blend of Incan and colonial architecture with luxurious amenities.
   - Amenities: Full-service spa, gourmet restaurants, and beautifully appointed rooms.
   - Highlight: The hotel's rich history and elegant design provide a unique cultural experience.

★ Sacred Valley

1. Tambo del Inka, a Luxury Collection Resort & Spa:
   - Overview: Nestled in the Sacred Valley, this resort offers stunning views, spacious accommodations, and easy access to nearby ruins and markets.
   - Amenities: Full-service spa, heated indoor/outdoor pool, and an exquisite restaurant.
   - Highlight: The resort's location along the Urubamba River makes it an ideal base for exploring the Sacred Valley and Machu Picchu.

2. Belmond Rio Sagrado:
   - Overview: Located along the banks of the Urubamba River, this hotel offers serene and luxurious accommodations.
   - Amenities: Spa, heated outdoor pool, gourmet dining, and private villas.

- Highlight: The tranquil setting and breathtaking natural beauty provide a peaceful escape from the hustle and bustle of city life.

★ Machu Picchu

1. Inkaterra Machu Picchu Pueblo Hotel:
- Overview: Situated in the cloud forest near the base of Machu Picchu, this eco-friendly hotel offers a luxurious and immersive experience.
- Amenities: Spa, orchid garden, bird-watching tours, and gourmet dining.
- Highlight: The property's lush surroundings and close proximity to Machu Picchu make it an exceptional choice for nature lovers.

2. Sumaq Machu Picchu Hotel:
- Overview: A luxurious hotel located near the town of Aguas Calientes, offering stunning views and top-notch amenities.
- Amenities: Full-service spa, gourmet Peruvian cuisine, and guided tours to Machu Picchu.
- Highlight: The hotel's focus on Andean culture and hospitality ensures an authentic and enriching experience.

★ Arequipa

1. CIRQA - Relais & Châteaux:
 - Overview: A luxurious boutique hotel housed in a former monastery, blending historic charm with modern comfort.
 - Amenities: Personalized service, exquisite dining, and beautifully restored rooms.
 - Highlight: The hotel's intimate setting and historical significance provide a unique and memorable stay.

★ Amazon Rainforest

1. Inkaterra Reserva Amazónica:
 - Overview: An eco-luxury lodge located in the heart of the Amazon, offering immersive jungle experiences with comfort and style.
 - Amenities: Private cabins, guided jungle excursions, spa services, and fine dining.
 - Highlight: The lodge's commitment to sustainability and conservation enhances the authenticity of the Amazon experience.

2. Tambopata Research Center:
 - Overview: A remote eco-lodge offering luxury accommodations and unparalleled access to wildlife and research activities.

- Amenities: Comfortable rooms, guided tours, and opportunities to participate in conservation efforts.
  - Highlight: The lodge's secluded location allows for an intimate connection with the surrounding rainforest and its inhabitants.

Staying at one of these luxury hotels not only provides a comfortable and lavish retreat but also offers a unique way to experience Peru's rich cultural and natural heritage. Each property combines exceptional service with a deep respect for the local environment and traditions, ensuring an unforgettable stay.

Mid-Range Hotels

For travelers seeking comfortable and affordable accommodations, Peru offers a variety of midrange hotels that provide excellent value without compromising on quality or amenities. Here are some top midrange hotel options in key destinations across the country:

- Lima

1. Casa Andina Select Miraflores:
   - Overview: Located in the heart of Miraflores, this hotel offers modern comforts and is within walking distance of popular attractions, shops, and restaurants.
   - Amenities: Fitness center, restaurant, free Wi-Fi, and business center.
   - Highlight: The convenient location makes it easy to explore Lima's vibrant neighborhoods.

2. Ibis Larco Miraflores:
   - Overview: A budget-friendly option with clean, modern rooms and easy access to the beachfront and Larcomar shopping center.
   - Amenities: On-site restaurant, bar, free Wi-Fi, and 24-hour front desk service.
   - Highlight: Known for its consistent quality and excellent location.

- Cusco

1. Tierra Viva Cusco Centro:

- Overview: A charming hotel located close to Cusco's main square, offering a blend of modern amenities and traditional Andean décor.
   - Amenities: Complimentary breakfast, free Wi-Fi, and airport shuttle service.
   - Highlight: The cozy atmosphere and friendly staff make it a popular choice among travelers.

2. El Mercado:
   - Overview: This boutique hotel, housed in a former marketplace, combines rustic charm with modern comforts.
   - Amenities: Complimentary breakfast, on-site restaurant, and free Wi-Fi.
   - Highlight: The unique design and central location provide an authentic Cusco experience.

- Sacred Valley

1. Hotel Pakaritampu:
   - Overview: Located in Ollantaytambo, this hotel offers a peaceful retreat with beautiful gardens and traditional Andean architecture.
   - Amenities: Restaurant, bar, free Wi-Fi, and tour services.
   - Highlight: The serene setting and proximity to the Ollantaytambo ruins make it an ideal base for exploring the Sacred Valley.

2. Casa Andina Standard Sacred Valley:
   - Overview: A comfortable hotel set amidst beautiful landscapes, offering easy access to the region's attractions.
   - Amenities: Restaurant, free Wi-Fi, and outdoor activities.
   - Highlight: The scenic location and warm hospitality ensure a pleasant stay.

- Arequipa

1. Casa Andina Standard Arequipa:
   - Overview: Located near the historic center, this hotel offers comfortable accommodations with modern amenities.
   - Amenities: Restaurant, free Wi-Fi, and complimentary breakfast.
   - Highlight: The hotel's proximity to Arequipa's main attractions makes it a convenient choice for visitors.

2. La Hostería:
   - Overview: A charming colonial-style hotel with cozy rooms and a beautiful courtyard.
   - Amenities: Spa, free Wi-Fi, and complimentary breakfast.
   - Highlight: The hotel's historic ambiance and relaxing atmosphere provide a unique experience.

- Amazon Rainforest

1. EcoAmazonia Lodge:
 - Overview: An eco-friendly lodge located in the Tambopata National Reserve, offering comfortable accommodations in the heart of the rainforest.
 - Amenities: Guided jungle tours, restaurant, and free Wi-Fi in common areas.
 - Highlight: The lodge's commitment to sustainability and its immersive jungle experience make it a standout choice.

2. Hacienda Concepción by Inkaterra:
 - Overview: A rustic yet comfortable lodge near Puerto Maldonado, providing a range of activities and excursions.
 - Amenities: Restaurant, guided tours, and wellness facilities.
 - Highlight: The lodge's location on the banks of the Madre de Dios River offers easy access to the surrounding natural beauty.

These midrange hotels provide a perfect balance of comfort, affordability, and convenience, ensuring a pleasant stay as you explore the wonders of Peru. Whether you're in the bustling city of Lima, the historic heart of Cusco, the serene Sacred Valley, the picturesque Arequipa, or the lush Amazon Rainforest, these accommodations offer excellent value and memorable experiences

Budget Hostels

Traveling to Peru on a budget doesn't mean you have to sacrifice comfort or a memorable experience. The country offers a variety of budget-friendly accommodations that provide clean, comfortable, and convenient stays without breaking the bank. Here are some top budget hotel options in key destinations across Peru:

- Lima

1. 1900 Hostel:
 - Overview: Located in the historic center of Lima, this hostel offers a friendly atmosphere and a variety of room options, from dormitories to private rooms.
   - Amenities: Free Wi-Fi, complimentary breakfast, shared kitchen, and a rooftop terrace.

- Highlight: The hostel's historic building and proximity to major attractions make it a popular choice among budget travelers.

2. The Lighthouse Bed and Breakfast:
  - Overview: A cozy B&B located in the Miraflores district, offering comfortable rooms at affordable rates.
  - Amenities: Complimentary breakfast, free Wi-Fi, and a communal kitchen.
  - Highlight: The B&B's warm hospitality and convenient location near parks and the coastline.

- Cusco

1. Pariwana Hostel Cusco:
  - Overview: A lively hostel with a great social atmosphere, located just a few blocks from Cusco's main square.
  - Amenities: Free Wi-Fi, complimentary breakfast, bar, and organized activities.
  - Highlight: The hostel's vibrant ambiance and the opportunity to meet fellow travelers.

2. El Tuco Hotel:
  - Overview: A family-run hotel offering clean, comfortable rooms and friendly service at reasonable prices.

- Amenities: Free Wi-Fi, complimentary breakfast, and a shared lounge.
   - Highlight: The hotel's homey atmosphere and helpful staff make it a comfortable base for exploring Cusco.

- **Sacred Valley**

1. Hostal Iskay:
   - Overview: Located in Ollantaytambo, this charming hostel offers rustic-style rooms with beautiful views of the surrounding mountains.
   - Amenities: Complimentary breakfast, free Wi-Fi, and tour services.
   - Highlight: The hostel's peaceful setting and proximity to the Ollantaytambo ruins.

2. Casa de Mama Valle:
   - Overview: A budget-friendly guesthouse in the heart of Urubamba, offering simple and clean accommodations.
   - Amenities: Free Wi-Fi, complimentary breakfast, and a communal kitchen.
   - Highlight: The guesthouse's central location and welcoming atmosphere.

- **Arequipa**

1. Misti House:
   - Overview: A budget hotel located near the historic center of Arequipa, offering basic and comfortable rooms.
   - Amenities: Free Wi-Fi, complimentary breakfast, and a rooftop terrace.
   - Highlight: The hotel's affordability and convenient location make it a great choice for budget travelers.

2. Bothy Hostel Arequipa:
   - Overview: A friendly hostel with a mix of dormitory and private rooms, located close to the main square.
   - Amenities: Free Wi-Fi, complimentary breakfast, bar, and a rooftop terrace with views of the city.
   - Highlight: The hostel's social atmosphere and organized activities.

- Amazon Rainforest

1. Monte Amazonico Lodge:
   - Overview: An affordable eco-lodge located near Puerto Maldonado, offering basic but comfortable accommodations in the heart of the rainforest.
   - Amenities: Guided jungle tours, restaurant, and free Wi-Fi in common areas.

- Highlight: The lodge's location provides easy access to the surrounding natural beauty and wildlife.

2. Tambopata Ecolodge:
   - Overview: A budget-friendly ecolodge in the Tambopata National Reserve, offering rustic cabins and a true jungle experience.
   - Amenities: Guided tours, restaurant, and sustainable practices.
   - Highlight: The lodge's emphasis on eco-tourism and its immersive setting in the Amazon.

These budget hotels provide great value for money, ensuring you can enjoy your trip to Peru without stretching your budget. From the bustling city of Lima to the historic charm of Cusco, the serene Sacred Valley, the picturesque Arequipa, and the lush Amazon Rainforest, these accommodations offer comfort, convenience, and a welcoming atmosphere.

Unique Stays

For travelers seeking a distinctive and memorable experience, Peru offers a variety of unique accommodations that go beyond the typical hotel stay. Whether you're looking to immerse yourself in nature, connect with local culture, or simply enjoy a one-of-a-kind setting, these unique stays provide an unforgettable experience.

- **Sacred Valley**

1. Skylodge Adventure Suites:
   - Overview: Suspended on a cliffside, these transparent pods offer breathtaking views of the Sacred Valley by day and a canopy of stars by night.
   - Amenities: Comfortable beds, private bathroom, and breakfast and dinner served in your pod.
   - Highlight: The adventure begins with a climb or hike to reach your pod, adding an exhilarating element to your stay.

2. Andenia Hotel Boutique:
   - Overview: Set amidst lush gardens and mountain views, this boutique hotel blends rustic charm with modern comforts.
   - Amenities: Spacious rooms, personalized service, and guided tours of the Sacred Valley.

- Highlight: The hotel's serene setting and attention to detail provide a tranquil retreat.

- **Amazon Rainforest**

1. Treehouse Lodge:
   - Overview: Located in the heart of the Amazon, this lodge offers guests the unique experience of staying in treehouses elevated above the jungle floor.
   - Amenities: Private treehouses, guided jungle tours, and all-inclusive meals.
   - Highlight: Fall asleep to the sounds of the rainforest and wake up to views of the canopy.

2. Tambopata Research Center:
   - Overview: A remote eco-lodge focused on conservation and research, providing an immersive jungle experience.
   - Amenities: Comfortable rooms, guided wildlife tours, and opportunities to engage with researchers.
   - Highlight: The lodge's location within the Tambopata National Reserve allows for unparalleled wildlife viewing.

- **Lake Titicaca**

1. Titilaka Lodge:

- Overview: An all-inclusive luxury lodge on the shores of Lake Titicaca, offering stunning views and cultural immersion.
   - Amenities: Elegant rooms, gourmet dining, and a range of excursions including visits to the floating islands.
   - Highlight: The lodge's remote location provides a peaceful and immersive experience of Lake Titicaca.

2. Uros Floating Islands Homestay:
   - Overview: Experience life on the floating islands of the Uros people by staying in a traditional reed house.
   - Amenities: Basic accommodations, homemade meals, and cultural activities with your host family.
   - Highlight: Gain insight into the unique way of life of the Uros community and their sustainable practices.

- Colca Canyon

1. Colca Lodge Spa & Hot Springs:
   - Overview: Nestled in the Colca Valley, this lodge offers rustic elegance and natural hot springs for relaxation.
   - Amenities: Cozy rooms, spa services, and thermal baths.

- Highlight: The lodge's hot springs, set amidst stunning canyon scenery, provide a perfect way to unwind after a day of exploration.

2. Killawasi Lodge:
 - Overview: A charming lodge located in the heart of Colca Valley, offering comfortable rooms and personalized service.
 - Amenities: Restaurant, guided tours, and free Wi-Fi.
 - Highlight: The lodge's beautiful gardens and close proximity to the canyon make it an ideal base for exploring the area.

- Arequipa

1. Cirqa - Relais & Châteaux:
 - Overview: A boutique hotel housed in a former monastery, blending historic charm with modern luxury.
 - Amenities: Personalized service, exquisite dining, and beautifully restored rooms.
 - Highlight: The hotel's intimate setting and historical significance provide a unique and memorable stay.

These unique accommodations offer not just a place to rest, but an experience that connects you more deeply with Peru's landscapes, cultures, and heritage. Whether you're sleeping in a treehouse in the Amazon, climbing to your pod in the Sacred Valley, or staying with a local family on Lake Titicaca, these stays promise memories that will last a lifetime.

Booking Tips and Recommendations

Planning a trip to Peru involves more than just choosing destinations and accommodations. To ensure a smooth and enjoyable experience, here are some essential booking tips and recommendations:

➢ Research and Plan Ahead

1. High Season vs. Low Season:
   - High Season (May to September): This is the peak tourist season, especially in popular areas like Machu Picchu and Cusco. Book accommodations, flights, and tours well in advance to secure your preferred options and take advantage of early booking discounts.
   - Low Season (November to March): This period sees fewer tourists, and you might find better deals on hotels and tours. However, be mindful of the rainy season in the highlands and the Amazon.

2. Travel Guides and Reviews:

- Read Reviews: Use websites like TripAdvisor and booking platforms to read reviews and get insights from fellow travelers.

- Local Blogs and Forums: Check out travel blogs and forums for firsthand experiences and recommendations specific to Peru.

➢ Booking Accommodations

1. Hotels and Hostels:

- Direct Booking: Sometimes booking directly through a hotel's website can provide better rates and exclusive offers compared to third-party booking sites.

- Booking Platforms: Use reputable platforms like Booking.com or Expedia to compare prices, read reviews, and find deals.

2. Eco-Lodges and Unique Stays:

- Early Reservations: For unique stays like the Skylodge Adventure Suites or Amazon eco-lodges, book well in advance as these accommodations can fill up quickly.

- Special Requests: If you have specific needs or requests (e.g., dietary restrictions, accessibility), contact the accommodation directly to ensure they can accommodate you.

➢ Flights and Transportation

1. Flexible Dates:
 - Use Flexible Date Search: When booking flights, use flexible date search options to find the best rates. Flying mid-week often offers cheaper fares than weekends.
 - Seasonal Sales: Keep an eye out for airline sales and special offers, especially during holiday seasons or off-peak times.

2. Connecting Flights:
 - International Connections: If there are no direct flights from your city to Peru, consider booking connecting flights through major hubs like Miami, Bogotá, or Santiago.
 - Domestic Flights: For traveling within Peru, domestic flights can be booked with airlines like LATAM, Avianca, or Sky Airline. Booking in advance can secure lower fares.

➢ Tours and Excursions

1. Reputable Tour Operators:
 - Research Operators: Choose reputable tour operators with good reviews for excursions like the Inca Trail, Amazon tours, and Sacred Valley trips.

Look for operators who emphasize sustainability and support local communities.

- Book in Advance: Popular tours such as the Inca Trail require permits that sell out months in advance. Secure your spot early to avoid disappointment.

2. Customizable Tours:
    - Personalized Experiences: Consider customizable tours that allow you to tailor the itinerary to your interests and preferences. This can enhance your experience and ensure you see the sites that matter most to you.

➢ Budgeting and Payments

1. Currency and Payments:
- Local Currency: The Peruvian Sol (PEN) is the local currency. While major cities accept credit cards, it's advisable to carry cash for smaller towns and markets.
- Exchange Rates: Use official currency exchange offices or ATMs to get the best rates. Avoid changing money at airports or hotels, where rates are typically less favorable.

2. Tipping:

- General Practice: Tipping is customary in Peru, especially in restaurants and for tour guides. A standard tip is around 10% of the bill in restaurants and $5-$10 USD per day for guides.

Health and Safety

1. Travel Insurance:
   - Comprehensive Coverage: Purchase travel insurance that covers medical emergencies, trip cancellations, and lost luggage. Make sure it includes coverage for high-altitude activities if you plan to hike in the Andes.
   - Emergency Contact: Keep a copy of your insurance policy and emergency contact numbers with you at all times.

2. Vaccinations and Health Precautions:
   - Vaccinations: Ensure you have the necessary vaccinations, such as yellow fever, especially if traveling to the Amazon region.
   - Health Precautions: Pack a basic first aid kit, including medication for altitude sickness, insect repellent, and any personal prescriptions.

By following these booking tips and recommendations, you'll be well-prepared for your trip to Peru. Careful planning and thoughtful choices can enhance your travel experience, allowing you to focus on enjoying the rich culture, stunning landscapes, and warm hospitality that Peru has to offer.

Chapter 6: Food and Drink

Must-Try Dishes

Peruvian cuisine is a vibrant fusion of indigenous ingredients and diverse cultural influences, including Spanish, African, Chinese, and Japanese. This culinary melting pot has given rise to some of the most flavorful and unique dishes in the world. Here are some must-try dishes that you shouldn't miss during your visit to Peru:

1. Ceviche

- Overview: Ceviche is Peru's national dish, consisting of fresh raw fish marinated in citrus juices, typically lime or lemon. The acidity "cooks" the fish, resulting in a flavorful and refreshing dish.

- Ingredients: Fresh fish (such as sea bass or tilapia), lime juice, red onions, cilantro, aji amarillo (yellow chili pepper), and salt.
- Serving: It's usually served with sides such as sweet potato, corn, and cancha (toasted corn kernels).

2. Lomo Saltado

- Overview: A popular stir-fry dish that reflects Peru's Chinese influence. It combines marinated strips of beef with vegetables and soy sauce, served with fried potatoes and rice.
- Ingredients: Beef tenderloin, red onions, tomatoes, soy sauce, vinegar, aji amarillo, and cilantro.
- Flavor: The combination of flavors is both savory and slightly tangy, with a hint of spice from the aji amarillo.

3. Aji de Gallina

- Overview: This creamy chicken stew is a comforting and flavorful dish, made with shredded chicken in a rich, spicy sauce.

- Ingredients: Shredded chicken, aji amarillo paste, evaporated milk, bread, garlic, pecans or walnuts, and Parmesan cheese.
- Serving: Typically served with boiled potatoes, rice, and black olives.

4. Anticuchos

- Overview: These are skewers of marinated and grilled meat, often beef heart, that are a popular street food in Peru.
- Ingredients: Beef heart (or other meats), garlic, vinegar, cumin, aji panca (red chili pepper), and salt.
- Flavor: The meat is tender and flavorful, with a smoky char from the grill. It is usually served with potatoes and a spicy sauce.

5. Rocoto Relleno

- Overview: A traditional dish from Arequipa, rocoto relleno features spicy red peppers stuffed with a savory meat mixture and topped with cheese.
- Ingredients: Rocoto peppers, ground beef or pork, onions, garlic, olives, hard-boiled eggs, and cheese.
- Preparation: The peppers are typically baked until the cheese is melted and the filling is cooked through.

6. Papa a la Huancaína

- Overview: This popular appetizer consists of boiled potatoes served with a spicy, creamy sauce made from cheese, aji amarillo, and milk.
- Ingredients: Potatoes, aji amarillo paste, queso fresco (fresh cheese), evaporated milk, garlic, and salt.
- Serving: The dish is often garnished with hard-boiled eggs and black olives.

7. Causa Rellena

- Overview: Causa is a layered potato dish that can be served cold or at room temperature. It features mashed potatoes flavored with lime and aji amarillo, layered with various fillings.
- Ingredients: Potatoes, lime juice, aji amarillo, mayonnaise, avocado, chicken or tuna, and vegetables.
- Variations: Fillings can vary widely, including combinations of chicken, tuna, avocado, and vegetables, making it a versatile and colorful dish.

8. Chupe de Camarones

- Overview: A rich and hearty shrimp soup from Arequipa, made with shrimp, potatoes, corn, and a creamy broth.
- Ingredients: Shrimp, potatoes, corn, aji amarillo, milk or cream, cheese, and eggs.
- Flavor: The soup is creamy and savory, with a mild heat from the aji amarillo.

9. Picarones

- Overview: These sweet, deep-fried doughnuts are made from a mix of squash and sweet potato, served with a syrup made from chancaca (molasses).
- Ingredients: Squash, sweet potato, flour, yeast, sugar, and chancaca syrup.
- Taste: They are crispy on the outside and soft on the inside, with a sweet and slightly spiced flavor.

10. Pollo a la Brasa

- Overview: One of Peru's most beloved dishes, this rotisserie chicken is marinated in a flavorful blend of spices and herbs, then roasted to perfection.
- Ingredients: Whole chicken, garlic, cumin, paprika, vinegar, and soy sauce.

- Serving: Typically served with French fries and a variety of dipping sauces, such as aji amarillo or huacatay (black mint).

These must-try dishes are just a glimpse into the rich and diverse culinary landscape of Peru. Each dish tells a story of the country's history, culture, and traditions, making every meal a unique and memorable experience.

Top Restaurants in Major Cities

- Lima

1. Central Restaurant - Known for its innovative Peruvian cuisine.
2. Maido - Offers exquisite haute Nikkei cuisine.
3. Astrid y Gastón - A culinary gem in Lima's gastronomic scene.
4. La Mar - Premier destination for ceviche.
5. Panchita - Famous for its delicious Peruvian comfort food.

- Cusco

1. MAP Café - Located in the Museo de Arte Precolombino.
2. Casa Carbajal Restaurante - Offers a fine dining experience.
3. Chicha - By renowned chef Gastón Acurio.
4. Cicciolina - Known for its contemporary fusion cuisine.
5. San Pedro Market - A must-visit for authentic local dishes like cuy.

- Arequipa

1. La Nueva Palomino - Famous for its traditional Peruvian dishes.
2. Chicha Perú - Offers a variety of Peruvian cuisine.
3. Donde Sol - Known for its beautiful views and delicious food.
4. La Bodega de Mario - A great spot for local cuisine.
5. El Pollo del Cuzco - Popular for its roasted chicken.

Local Beverages

Peruvian cuisine is not just about the food; it also features a rich variety of beverages, both traditional and modern. Here are some of the must-try local drinks that offer a taste of Peru's diverse culture and history:

1. Pisco Sour

- Overview: The Pisco Sour is Peru's national cocktail, celebrated for its tangy and refreshing flavor.
- Ingredients: Pisco (a type of brandy), lime juice, simple syrup, egg white, and Angostura bitters.
- Flavor: The drink has a perfect balance of sweet, sour, and frothy textures, with a slight bitterness from the Angostura bitters.
- Serving: Traditionally served in a short glass and garnished with a dash of bitters on the frothy egg white.

2. Chicha Morada

- Overview: Chicha Morada is a non-alcoholic traditional drink made from purple corn.
- Ingredients: Purple corn, pineapple, cinnamon, clove, sugar, and lime juice.
- Flavor: It has a sweet and slightly tangy flavor with a hint of spices from the cinnamon and clove.
- Serving: Usually served chilled, making it a refreshing beverage on a hot day.

3. Inca Kola

- Overview: Often referred to as "the golden kola," Inca Kola is a popular soft drink in Peru.
- Ingredients: Carbonated water, sugar, lemon verbena extract, and artificial coloring.
- Flavor: It has a sweet, bubblegum-like taste that is unique and quite distinct from traditional colas.
- Popularity: Inca Kola is a national favorite and is often enjoyed with meals.

4. Chicha de Jora

- Overview: Chicha de Jora is a traditional fermented corn beer with ancient origins in Inca culture.
- Ingredients: Jora corn, water, and sometimes fruit or spices for flavor.
- Flavor: The drink has a mildly alcoholic content and a slightly sour taste.
- Serving: Traditionally served in a clay pot or ceramic cup.

5. Emoliente

- Overview: Emoliente is a popular herbal tea, particularly enjoyed during the cooler months.

- Ingredients: A blend of herbs such as barley, flaxseed, alfalfa, and a variety of medicinal plants.
- Flavor: It has a soothing, slightly sweet taste, often enhanced with honey and lemon.
- Health Benefits: Emoliente is believed to have various health benefits, including aiding digestion and boosting the immune system.

6. Mate de Coca

- Overview: Mate de Coca is a herbal tea made from coca leaves, widely consumed in the Andean regions.
- Ingredients: Coca leaves and hot water.
- Flavor: The tea has a mild, earthy flavor similar to green tea.
- Benefits: It is commonly drunk to alleviate altitude sickness and boost energy levels.

7. Aguaje Juice

- Overview: Made from the aguaje fruit found in the Amazon Rainforest, this juice is both nutritious and delicious.
- Ingredients: Aguaje fruit, water, and sugar.
- Flavor: It has a sweet and slightly tart taste, often enjoyed as a refreshing drink.

- Nutritional Value: The fruit is rich in vitamins A and C, providing numerous health benefits.

8. Chapo

- Overview: Chapo is a traditional drink from the Amazon region made from ripe plantains.
- Ingredients: Ripe plantains, water, and sugar.
- Flavor: It has a sweet and creamy consistency, similar to a banana smoothie.
- Serving: Often enjoyed as a breakfast drink or a snack.

9. Peruvian Craft Beer

- Overview: The craft beer scene in Peru has been growing, with many local breweries producing unique and flavorful beers.
- Types: A variety of styles including pale ales, IPAs, stouts, and lagers, often incorporating local ingredients.
- Popular Breweries: Sierra Andina, Cervecería del Valle Sagrado, and Cerveza Zenith are among the notable breweries.

10. Refresco de Cebada

- Overview: Refresco de Cebada is a traditional barley-based drink, often consumed as a refreshing beverage.
- Ingredients: Barley, sugar, lemon juice, and spices.
- Flavor: It has a light, slightly sweet taste with a hint of citrus.
- Serving: Typically served cold, making it a popular drink during warm weather.

These local beverages offer a taste of Peru's rich culinary heritage and provide a refreshing complement to the country's diverse cuisine. Whether you're sipping on a Pisco Sour or enjoying a glass of Chicha Morada, these drinks are sure to enhance your Peruvian experience.

Food Tours and Culinary Experiences

Peru's rich culinary heritage and diverse food scene make it a perfect destination for food enthusiasts. Embarking on a food tour or engaging in culinary experiences is a fantastic way to dive deeper into the flavors and traditions of Peruvian cuisine. Here are some popular food tours and culinary activities you can enjoy in Peru:

- Lima

1. Lima Gourmet Company:
   - Overview: This tour offers a blend of traditional and contemporary Peruvian cuisine, showcasing the best of Lima's culinary scene.
   - Highlights: Visit local markets, taste street food, dine at top restaurants, and learn about the history and ingredients of Peruvian dishes.
   - Duration: Half-day and full-day tours available.

2. Exquisito Perú:
   - Overview: Exquisito Perú offers a variety of food tours that take you through different neighborhoods of Lima.
   - Highlights: Sample ceviche, pisco sours, and other local delicacies while exploring historic districts like Barranco and Miraflores.
   - Specialty Tours: Options include a market tour with a cooking class, a street food tour, and a gourmet tour.

3. Market Tours and Cooking Classes:
   - Overview: Many local chefs and cooking schools offer tours of Lima's bustling markets followed by hands-on cooking classes.

- Highlights: Learn to prepare classic Peruvian dishes like ceviche, lomo saltado, and causa. Classes often include insights into local ingredients and culinary techniques.

- Cusco

1. Cusco Culinary:
 - Overview: This food tour company offers immersive culinary experiences in Cusco, including market visits and cooking classes.
 - Highlights: Explore San Pedro Market, learn to prepare traditional dishes, and enjoy a meal with fellow food enthusiasts.
 - Signature Dishes: Try your hand at making dishes like quinoa soup, alpaca steaks, and traditional Andean desserts.

2. Taste Peruvian:
 - Overview: Offers a combination of food tours and cooking classes in Cusco, perfect for foodies looking to explore Andean cuisine.
 - Highlights: Visit local markets, taste authentic street food, and participate in interactive cooking sessions with experienced chefs.

- Arequipa

1. Arequipa Food Tours:
   - Overview: Discover the flavors of Arequipa with guided food tours that take you through the city's historic center and its vibrant food scene.
   - Highlights: Sample rocoto relleno, chupe de camarones, and other Arequipeño specialties. Tours often include visits to traditional picanterías (local eateries).
   - Cultural Experience: Learn about the cultural significance and history behind Arequipa's unique dishes.

2. Cooking Classes:
   - Overview: Engage in cooking classes that highlight Arequipa's distinct cuisine. Local chefs guide you through the preparation of traditional dishes.
   - Highlights: Hands-on experience in making classic Arequipeño meals, followed by a shared meal with your group.

- **Amazon Rainforest**

1. Amazon Culinary Tours:
   - Overview: Explore the unique flavors of the Amazon with culinary tours that include visits to local markets and cooking demonstrations.

- Highlights: Taste exotic fruits, fish from the Amazon River, and traditional jungle dishes. Learn about the use of medicinal plants and herbs in Amazonian cuisine.

- Eco-Lodge Experiences: Many eco-lodges offer culinary experiences as part of their stay, where you can learn to cook using ingredients harvested from the rainforest.

2. Community-Based Tourism:

- Overview: Participate in community-based tourism initiatives that offer an authentic taste of Amazonian life.

- Highlights: Spend time with indigenous communities, learn about their traditional cooking methods, and enjoy meals prepared with locally sourced ingredients.

- Sacred Valley

1. Sacred Valley Culinary Tours:

- Overview: Discover the culinary delights of the Sacred Valley with guided tours that combine food tastings, market visits, and cooking classes.

- Highlights: Taste local specialties like choclo con queso (corn with cheese) and trout from the Urubamba River. Visit traditional Andean markets and farms.

- Interactive Experiences: Participate in Pachamanca, an ancient Incan cooking technique where food is cooked underground using hot stones.

2. Farm-to-Table Experiences:
   - Overview: Enjoy farm-to-table dining experiences that highlight the fresh, seasonal produce of the Sacred Valley.
   - Highlights: Tour organic farms, harvest your own ingredients, and enjoy meals prepared by local chefs using traditional methods.

These food tours and culinary experiences offer a delicious and educational way to explore Peru's diverse culinary landscape. Whether you're in Lima, Cusco, Arequipa, the Amazon Rainforest, or the Sacred Valley, these activities provide a deeper understanding of Peruvian culture and cuisine, leaving you with unforgettable memories and new cooking skills.

Chapter 7: Culture and Customs

Basic Language Phrases

When traveling to Peru, it's helpful to know some basic phrases in Spanish, the country's official language. This not only makes communication easier but also enriches your travel experience by allowing you to connect more authentically with locals. Here are some essential phrases to get you started:

> Greetings and Common Phrases

1. Hello: Hola
2. Good morning: Buenos días
3. Good afternoon: Buenas tardes
4. Good evening/night: Buenas noches
5. Goodbye: Adiós
6. Please: Por favor
7. Thank you: Gracias
8. You're welcome: De nada
9. Excuse me: Disculpe / Perdón
10. I'm sorry: Lo siento
11. Yes: Sí
12. No: No

Introductions

1. What is your name?: ¿Cuál es tu nombre? / ¿Cómo te llamas?
2. My name is...: Mi nombre es... / Me llamo...
3. Nice to meet you: Mucho gusto

Basic Conversation

1. How are you?: ¿Cómo estás?
2. I'm fine, thank you: Estoy bien, gracias
3. Where are you from?: ¿De dónde eres?
4. I am from...: Soy de...
5. Do you speak English?: ¿Hablas inglés?
6. I don't understand: No entiendo
7. Can you help me?: ¿Puedes ayudarme?
8. Where is the bathroom?: ¿Dónde está el baño?
9. How much does it cost?: ¿Cuánto cuesta?

Directions

1. Left: Izquierda
2. Right: Derecha
3. Straight ahead: Todo recto
4. Near: Cerca
5. Far: Lejos
6. Where is...?: ¿Dónde está...?
7. How do I get to...?: ¿Cómo llego a...?

Dining

1. A table for two, please: Una mesa para dos, por favor
2. I would like...: Quisiera...
3. The menu, please: El menú, por favor
4. Check, please: La cuenta, por favor
5. Delicious: Delicioso

Shopping

1. How much is this?: ¿Cuánto cuesta esto?
2. I would like to buy...: Quisiera comprar...
3. Can you give me a discount?: ¿Me puede dar un descuento?
4. That's too expensive: Es muy caro
5. Do you accept credit cards?: ¿Aceptan tarjetas de crédito?

Transportation

1. Taxi: Taxi
2. Bus: Autobús
3. Train: Tren
4. Airport: Aeropuerto
5. Station: Estación
6. Ticket: Boleto

7. Where can I buy a ticket?: ¿Dónde puedo comprar un boleto?

Emergencies

1. Help!: ¡Ayuda!
2. Call a doctor!: ¡Llama a un doctor!
3. I need a doctor: Necesito un doctor
4. Police: Policía
5. Fire: Fuego

Learning these basic phrases will help you navigate your travels in Peru with greater ease and show respect for the local culture. Even if you're not fluent, making an effort to speak the local language is always appreciated and can lead to more enriching interactions.

Etiquette and Social Customs

Understanding local etiquette and social customs can greatly enhance your travel experience and help you connect more deeply with the people of Peru. Here are some key aspects of Peruvian etiquette and social customs to keep in mind:

- **Greetings**

1. Handshakes: A firm handshake with direct eye contact is the most common form of greeting in Peru. Men typically greet each other with a handshake, while women may exchange a light handshake or a kiss on the cheek.
2. Kiss on the Cheek: In more casual settings, it's common for women to greet each other and men with a single kiss on the right cheek. This is more common among friends and family.
3. Formal Address: When addressing someone, especially in formal or business settings, use "Señor" (Mr.), "Señora" (Mrs.), or "Señorita" (Miss) followed by their last name.

- **Social Interactions**

1. Personal Space: Peruvians may stand closer to each other during conversations than what some Westerners are accustomed to. This is a sign of friendliness rather than intrusion.
2. Politeness: Being polite and showing respect is very important. Always use "please" (por favor) and "thank you" (gracias) in your interactions.
3. Punctuality: While punctuality is valued in business settings, social gatherings in Peru often have a more relaxed attitude towards time. It's not

uncommon for events to start later than the scheduled time.

- Dining Etiquette

1. Table Manners: When invited to a Peruvian home, it's polite to wait for the host to indicate where to sit and when to start eating. Always keep your hands visible but not resting on the table.
2. Use of Utensils: Peruvians typically use a knife and fork for most meals. It is polite to finish everything on your plate as it shows appreciation for the meal.
3. Complimenting the Food: It's customary to compliment the host on the food. Simple phrases like "Está delicioso" (It's delicious) are appreciated.

- Gift Giving

1. Gifts: If you are invited to a Peruvian home, it's thoughtful to bring a small gift such as flowers, chocolates, or a bottle of wine. Avoid giving overly expensive gifts, as it may be seen as an attempt to impress.
2. Receiving Gifts: When receiving a gift, it is polite to open it immediately and express your gratitude.

- Dress Code

1. Casual Wear: Casual dress is acceptable for most everyday activities. However, when visiting religious sites or attending formal events, more conservative attire is recommended.
2. Business Attire: In business settings, men typically wear suits and ties, while women wear professional dresses or suits. It's important to dress smartly and professionally.

- Respect for Traditions and Customs

1. Religious Respect: Peru is predominantly Catholic, and religious traditions and festivals are an important part of the culture. Show respect by dressing modestly and behaving respectfully when visiting churches and participating in religious events.
2. Indigenous Cultures: Peru is home to many indigenous communities with distinct customs and traditions. Always show respect and ask for permission before taking photos of people or participating in cultural activities.

- Tipping

1. Restaurants: In more upscale restaurants, a 10% tip is appreciated if it's not already included in the

bill. For casual eateries and cafes, rounding up the bill or leaving a small tip is common.

2. Hotels: It is customary to tip bellboys and housekeeping staff a few soles for their services.

3. Tour Guides and Drivers: Tipping tour guides and drivers is common practice. A tip of 10-20 soles per day is generally appreciated.

Understanding and respecting these social customs and etiquette can help you navigate your interactions in Peru with confidence and grace. By showing respect for local traditions and being mindful of cultural norms, you'll enrich your travel experience and build positive relationships with the people you meet.

Festivals and Celebrations

Peru is a country rich in cultural traditions, and its festivals and celebrations reflect the diverse heritage and vibrant spirit of its people. From religious ceremonies to traditional Andean rituals, here are some of the most notable festivals and celebrations you can experience in Peru:

- **Inti Raymi (Festival of the Sun)**

- When: June 24th

- Where: Cusco
- Overview: Inti Raymi is one of the most important and elaborate Inca festivals, held to honor the sun god, Inti. It marks the winter solstice and the Incan New Year.
- Celebrations: The festival includes a grand procession, colorful costumes, traditional music, and dance performances. The main event takes place at the historic Sacsayhuamán fortress, where a re-enactment of the ancient ceremonies is performed.
- Highlights: Witnessing the re-enactment of Incan rituals, enjoying traditional Andean music and dance, and experiencing the vibrant atmosphere in Cusco.

- Virgen de la Candelaria

- When: Early February
- Where: Puno
- Overview: This festival honors the Virgin of Candelaria, the patron saint of Puno. It is one of the largest and most colorful festivals in Peru, blending Catholic and indigenous traditions.
- Celebrations: The festivities include religious processions, folk dances, live music, and elaborate costumes. The main events are held at the Puno Cathedral and around Lake Titicaca.

- Highlights: The spectacular dance performances, vibrant costumes, and the fusion of cultural traditions.

- **Semana Santa (Holy Week)**

- When: The week leading up to Easter Sunday
- Where: Throughout Peru, with notable celebrations in Ayacucho and Cusco
- Overview: Semana Santa is a major religious festival that commemorates the passion, death, and resurrection of Jesus Christ.
- Celebrations: The week is marked by solemn religious processions, re-enactments of the Stations of the Cross, and special church services. Ayacucho is particularly known for its elaborate processions and candlelit ceremonies.
- Highlights: The moving religious processions, intricate flower carpets, and the spiritual ambiance.

- **Fiesta de San Juan**

- When: June 24th
- Where: Amazon region
- Overview: This festival celebrates the birth of St. John the Baptist and is one of the most important events in the Amazon region.

- Celebrations: Activities include traditional music and dance, feasting on local delicacies, and ritual bathing in rivers, which is believed to bring good luck and purification.
- Highlights: The vibrant music and dance, traditional Amazonian cuisine, and the communal river baths.

- **Corpus Christi**

- When: 60 days after Easter Sunday
- Where: Cusco
- Overview: Corpus Christi is a significant Catholic festival that celebrates the presence of the Eucharist. In Cusco, it is one of the most important religious events of the year.
- Celebrations: The main event is a grand procession featuring ornate religious statues carried through the streets of Cusco. The procession is accompanied by traditional music and dance.
- Highlights: The beautifully decorated statues, the lively atmosphere, and the display of religious devotion.

- **Señor de los Milagros (Lord of Miracles)**

- When: October

- Where: Lima
- Overview: Señor de los Milagros is one of the largest religious processions in the world, honoring a 17th-century mural of Christ that survived an earthquake.
- Celebrations: The month-long festivities include processions through the streets of Lima, with thousands of devotees dressed in purple. The central event is the procession of the image of the Señor de los Milagros.
- Highlights: The devotion of the participants, the sea of purple attire, and the deeply spiritual atmosphere.

- Carnaval

- When: February or March, before Lent
- Where: Throughout Peru, with notable celebrations in Cajamarca and Puno
- Overview: Carnaval is a festive season celebrated with exuberant parades, colorful costumes, music, and dance.
- Celebrations: Activities include water fights, dance competitions, and street parties. Cajamarca is known for its lively parades and masked dancers, while Puno celebrates with traditional Andean music and dance.

- Highlights: The joyous parades, the playful water fights, and the vibrant cultural displays.

These festivals and celebrations offer a unique insight into Peru's rich cultural tapestry and provide unforgettable experiences for travelers. Whether you're witnessing ancient Incan rituals, participating in colorful parades, or joining in solemn religious processions, Peru's festivals are a testament to the country's vibrant traditions and enduring spirit.

Chapter 8: Adventure Activities

Hiking Trails

Peru is a hiker's paradise, offering a diverse range of trails that traverse breathtaking landscapes, ancient ruins, and stunning mountain ranges. Whether you're an experienced trekker or a casual hiker, there's a trail for everyone. Here are some of the most iconic and rewarding hiking trails in Peru:

➢ **Inca Trail**

- Overview: The Inca Trail is one of the most famous and sought-after hikes in the world, leading to the ancient city of Machu Picchu.
- Distance: Approximately 26 miles (42 kilometers).
- Duration: 4 days and 3 nights.

- Highlights: The trail passes through diverse ecosystems, cloud forests, and several Inca ruins, culminating in the iconic Sun Gate (Inti Punku) with a stunning view of Machu Picchu.
- Difficulty: Moderate to challenging, with steep ascents and descents.
- Permits: Limited permits are issued each day, so advance booking is essential.

> ➢ Salkantay Trek

- Overview: An alternative to the Inca Trail, the Salkantay Trek offers a less crowded route with equally spectacular scenery.
- Distance: Approximately 46 miles (74 kilometers).
- Duration: 5 days and 4 nights.
- Highlights: The trek traverses high mountain passes, including the majestic Salkantay Pass at 15,200 feet (4,650 meters), and descends into lush cloud forests and tropical valleys.
- Difficulty: Challenging, due to high altitudes and varying terrains.
- Permits: No permits required, but booking with a reputable tour operator is recommended.

> ➢ Colca Canyon Trek

- Overview: The Colca Canyon is one of the deepest canyons in the world, offering dramatic landscapes and the opportunity to see the majestic Andean condor.
- Distance: Varies depending on the route, typically 12-25 miles (20-40 kilometers).
- Duration: 2 to 3 days.
- Highlights: Stunning canyon views, traditional villages, natural hot springs, and condor sightings.
- Difficulty: Moderate to challenging, with steep descents and ascents.
- Permits: No permits required.

> Ausangate Trek

- Overview: The Ausangate Trek is a high-altitude circuit around the sacred Ausangate Mountain, known for its pristine landscapes and colorful lakes.
- Distance: Approximately 43 miles (70 kilometers).
- Duration: 5 to 6 days.
- Highlights: Snow-capped peaks, vibrant glacial lakes, hot springs, and remote Andean villages.
- Difficulty: Challenging, with high altitudes and rugged terrains.
- Permits: No permits required, but hiring a local guide is recommended due to the remote nature of the trek.

➢ Lares Trek

- Overview: The Lares Trek offers a cultural experience, passing through traditional Andean communities and beautiful mountain scenery.
- Distance: Approximately 21 miles (33 kilometers).
- Duration: 3 days and 2 nights.
- Highlights: Interactions with local Quechua-speaking villagers, hot springs, and stunning views of the Andean mountains.
- Difficulty: Moderate, with some steep sections.
- Permits: No permits required.

➢ Huascarán National Park

- Overview: Located in the Cordillera Blanca, Huascarán National Park offers several trekking routes through some of the highest tropical mountains in the world.
- Notable Treks: The Santa Cruz Trek and the Laguna 69 Hike are among the most popular.
- Highlights: Snow-capped peaks, turquoise lakes, and diverse flora and fauna.
- Difficulty: Varies by trail, ranging from moderate to challenging.
- Permits: Entrance fee required for the park.

➢ Choquequirao Trek

- Overview: The Choquequirao Trek leads to the remote Inca ruins of Choquequirao, often referred to as the "sister city" of Machu Picchu.
- Distance: Approximately 39 miles (62 kilometers) round trip.
- Duration: 4 to 5 days.
- Highlights: The impressive Choquequirao ruins, stunning mountain scenery, and fewer crowds compared to the Inca Trail.
- Difficulty: Challenging, with steep and strenuous sections.
- Permits: No permits required.

> Cordillera Huayhuash

- Overview: The Cordillera Huayhuash trek is one of the most challenging and rewarding high-altitude treks in the world.
- Distance: Approximately 81 miles (130 kilometers).
- Duration: 10 to 12 days.
- Highlights: Dramatic mountain landscapes, turquoise lakes, glaciers, and remote Andean communities.
- Difficulty: Very challenging, suitable for experienced trekkers.
- Permits: Permits required for certain sections, and hiring a local guide is recommended.

Wildlife and Nature Tours

Peru is a country of incredible biodiversity, offering a wealth of opportunities to explore its rich natural landscapes and observe a variety of wildlife. Whether you're trekking through the Amazon Rainforest, exploring the Andes mountains, or visiting coastal reserves, there's something for every nature enthusiast. Here are some of the top wildlife and nature tours in Peru:

- **Amazon Rainforest Tours**

1. Tambopata National Reserve:
   - Overview: Located in southeastern Peru, Tambopata is a haven for wildlife, including jaguars, giant otters, macaws, and anacondas.
   - Highlights: Guided tours take you deep into the rainforest, offering activities like canopy walks, boat rides, and night safaris to spot nocturnal creatures.
   - Eco-Lodges: Many tours include stays at eco-lodges such as Posada Amazonas, Refugio Amazonas, and Tambopata Research Center, which offer immersive jungle experiences.

2. Manu National Park:
   - Overview: A UNESCO World Heritage site, Manu National Park is one of the most biodiverse areas on the planet.

- Highlights: Explore the park's varied ecosystems, from lowland rainforests to cloud forests. Spotting wildlife like capybaras, giant otters, and colorful birds is a common highlight.

   - Tour Options: Multi-day tours with experienced guides, offering river excursions, jungle treks, and visits to indigenous communities.

3. Pacaya-Samiria National Reserve:
   - Overview: Located in the northern Amazon near Iquitos, Pacaya-Samiria is the largest protected area in Peru.

   - Highlights: Known for its pink river dolphins, this reserve offers boat tours, canoe trips, and guided hikes to observe wildlife and explore flooded forests.

   - Eco-Lodges: Stay at remote lodges like the Muyuna Lodge or Delfin Amazon Cruises for a luxurious experience.

- Andean Wildlife Tours

1. Huascarán National Park:
   - Overview: Situated in the Cordillera Blanca, this park is home to some of the highest tropical mountains in the world.

   - Highlights: Trekking through the park offers views of snow-capped peaks, turquoise glacial lakes, and the chance to spot Andean condors, vicuñas, and spectacled bears.

- Popular Hikes: The Santa Cruz Trek and the hike to Laguna 69 are among the most popular.

2. Colca Canyon:

- Overview: One of the deepest canyons in the world, Colca Canyon is a prime location for observing Andean condors.

- Highlights: The Cruz del Condor viewpoint is famous for its condor sightings. The canyon's dramatic landscapes and traditional villages add to the experience.

- Tour Options: Day tours and multi-day treks are available, often including visits to hot springs and local markets.

- **Coastal and Marine Tours**

1. Ballestas Islands:

- Overview: Often referred to as the "Poor Man's Galapagos," the Ballestas Islands are teeming with marine wildlife.

- Highlights: Boat tours from Paracas take you to the islands, where you can see sea lions, Humboldt penguins, and a variety of seabirds.

- Additional Attractions: The nearby Paracas National Reserve offers stunning coastal landscapes and opportunities for birdwatching.

2. Paracas National Reserve:
  - Overview: This coastal reserve features desert landscapes, dramatic cliffs, and diverse marine life.
  - Highlights: Spot flamingos, dolphins, and sea turtles. The reserve's unique geology and archaeological sites add to the appeal.
  - Tour Options: Guided tours include boat trips, dune buggy adventures, and visits to ancient ruins.

- High Altitude Nature Tours

1. Lake Titicaca:
  - Overview: The highest navigable lake in the world, Lake Titicaca is known for its stunning beauty and cultural significance.
  - Highlights: Boat tours to the Uros Floating Islands and Taquile Island offer insights into traditional lifestyles and breathtaking landscapes.
  - Wildlife: The lake is home to unique species of frogs, birds, and fish.

2. Ausangate Trek:
  - Overview: This high-altitude trek around the sacred Ausangate Mountain offers spectacular

natural scenery and encounters with Andean wildlife.

 - Highlights: Spotting herds of alpacas and llamas, visiting colorful glacial lakes, and enjoying views of snow-capped peaks.

 - Tour Options: Guided treks range from 5 to 7 days, with options for camping or staying in traditional mountain lodges.

- Desert and Coastal Wildlife Tours

1. Nazca Lines and Huacachina:

 - Overview: Combine a flight over the mysterious Nazca Lines with a visit to the desert oasis of Huacachina.

 - Highlights: The Nazca Lines are ancient geoglyphs that can only be fully appreciated from the air. Huacachina offers sandboarding and dune buggy adventures.

 - Wildlife: While primarily known for its landscapes, the region also offers birdwatching opportunities in nearby wetlands.

These wildlife and nature tours provide incredible opportunities to explore Peru's diverse ecosystems and observe its rich array of wildlife. Whether you're navigating the dense Amazon Rainforest, trekking through the majestic Andes, or exploring the vibrant marine life along the coast, Peru's natural beauty promises unforgettable adventures.

Outdoor Sports

Peru is an adventurer's playground, offering a wide range of outdoor sports that take advantage of its diverse landscapes, from the towering Andes mountains to the vast Amazon rainforest and pristine coastal waters. Whether you're seeking thrilling challenges or leisurely outdoor activities, Peru has something for every outdoor enthusiast. Here are some of the top outdoor sports you can enjoy in Peru:

- Hiking and Trekking

1. Inca Trail:
   - Overview: One of the most famous hiking trails in the world, leading to the ancient city of Machu Picchu.
   - Highlights: Stunning scenery, ancient Inca ruins, and the iconic Sun Gate view of Machu Picchu.

2. Salkantay Trek:
   - Overview: An alternative to the Inca Trail, offering breathtaking views of snow-capped peaks and lush valleys.

- Highlights: High mountain passes, cloud forests, and diverse ecosystems.

3. Cordillera Huayhuash Trek:
  - Overview: A challenging high-altitude trek through the stunning Cordillera Huayhuash mountain range.
  - Highlights: Dramatic landscapes, turquoise lakes, and remote Andean villages.

- Mountain Biking

1. Sacred Valley:
  - Overview: Explore the Sacred Valley's picturesque landscapes and Inca ruins on two wheels.
  - Highlights: Trails that range from easy rides to challenging descents, passing through traditional villages and archaeological sites.

2. Colca Canyon:
  - Overview: Mountain biking in one of the world's deepest canyons offers thrilling descents and stunning views.
  - Highlights: Ride along canyon walls, through quaint villages, and enjoy the natural beauty of the region.

3. Lima Coast:
- Overview: Coastal bike rides offer scenic routes along Lima's cliffs and beaches.
- Highlights: The Malecon in Miraflores, which provides beautiful ocean views and a pleasant cycling path.

- Surfing

1. Máncora:
- Overview: A popular beach destination known for its consistent waves and relaxed atmosphere.
- Highlights: Warm waters, beginner-friendly surf schools, and vibrant nightlife.

2. Punta Hermosa:
- Overview: Located south of Lima, Punta Hermosa is known for its excellent surf breaks.
- Highlights: A variety of waves for different skill levels, including the famous La Isla and Pico Alto breaks.

3. Huanchaco:
- Overview: A historic fishing village turned surf town, famous for its traditional reed boats and consistent waves.
- Highlights: Long sandy beaches, surf schools, and a laid-back vibe.

- Rock Climbing

1. Hatun Machay:
- Overview: Known as the "Forest of Stones," Hatun Machay is a premier rock climbing destination in the Andes.
- Highlights: A variety of climbing routes for all skill levels, set amidst stunning rock formations and high-altitude landscapes.

2. Cusco Region:
- Overview: The Cusco region offers several rock climbing spots with breathtaking views of the Andes.
- Highlights: Climbing routes near the Sacred Valley, with opportunities to combine climbing with cultural exploration.

3. Lima Region:
- Overview: The limestone cliffs of Lima offer accessible climbing routes close to the city.
- Highlights: The La Molina and Marcahuasi areas provide a range of climbing challenges for enthusiasts.

- White-Water Rafting

1. Urubamba River:

- Overview: Experience the thrill of white-water rafting in the Sacred Valley.
- Highlights: Exciting rapids, beautiful scenery, and the chance to see Inca ruins from the river.

2. Apurímac River:
- Overview: Known for its challenging rapids, the Apurímac River offers one of the best white-water rafting experiences in Peru.
- Highlights: Class III to V rapids, remote canyon landscapes, and abundant wildlife.

3. Tambopata River:
- Overview: Combine rafting with a rainforest adventure in the Amazon.
- Highlights: Gentle rapids, lush jungle scenery, and opportunities for wildlife spotting.

- Paragliding

1. Lima - Miraflores:
- Overview: Soar over the cliffs of Miraflores and enjoy panoramic views of the Pacific Ocean.
- Highlights: Tandem paragliding flights from the Malecon, offering stunning aerial views of Lima's coastline.

2. Sacred Valley:

- Overview: Paragliding in the Sacred Valley offers breathtaking views of the Andes and Inca ruins.

- Highlights: Launch sites near Urubamba and Pisac, with experienced pilots offering tandem flights.

- Kayaking

1. Lake Titicaca:
- Overview: Paddle through the serene waters of the highest navigable lake in the world.

- Highlights: Kayak to the Uros Floating Islands, Taquile Island, and explore the unique cultural heritage of the lake's communities.

2. Amazon Rivers:
- Overview: Kayaking in the Amazon offers a unique way to explore the rainforest's waterways.

- Highlights: Paddle through tranquil streams, spot exotic wildlife, and immerse yourself in the lush jungle environment.

Peru's diverse landscapes provide endless opportunities for outdoor sports and adventure activities. Whether you're hiking ancient trails, surfing along the coast, or paragliding over stunning valleys, Peru promises thrilling experiences and unforgettable memories for outdoor enthusiasts.

Adventure Tour Operators

Peru is a land of adventure, offering a wide range of thrilling activities from hiking ancient trails to exploring the Amazon rainforest. To make the most of your adventure, it's important to choose a reliable and reputable tour operator. Here are some of the top adventure tour operators in Peru, known for their expertise, safety standards, and commitment to sustainable tourism:

- G Adventures

- Overview: G Adventures is a renowned global adventure travel company that offers small group tours focused on authentic and immersive experiences.
- Specialties: Multi-day treks, cultural tours, and wildlife expeditions.
- Popular Tours: Inca Trail to Machu Picchu, Amazon Riverboat Adventure, and the Highlights of Peru tour.
- Sustainability: Committed to responsible travel, G Adventures supports local communities and environmental conservation.

- **Intrepid Travel**

- Overview: Intrepid Travel specializes in small group adventures that provide an in-depth cultural experience.
- Specialties: Hiking, biking, and cultural immersion tours.
- Popular Tours: Inca Trail Express, Sacred Valley and Lares Trek, and the Peru Real Food Adventure.
- Sustainability: Intrepid Travel emphasizes sustainable travel practices and supports local economies through community-based tourism.

- **Peru Hop**

- Overview: Peru Hop offers flexible hop-on, hop-off bus tours that allow travelers to explore Peru at their own pace.
- Specialties: Adventure tours, cultural experiences, and flexible itineraries.
- Popular Tours: Full South to Cusco, Cusco to La Paz, and Lima to Arequipa routes.
- Unique Features: Free extras like sandboarding in Huacachina, boat tours to the Ballestas Islands, and visits to the Nazca Lines.

- **Mountain Lodges of Peru**

- Overview: Mountain Lodges of Peru offers luxury trekking experiences with stays in comfortable lodges along the way.
- Specialties: High-end trekking tours with cultural immersion and comfort.
- Popular Tours: Salkantay Trek to Machu Picchu, Sacred Valley and Lares Adventure, and the Grand Andean Experience.
- Highlights: Combining adventure with luxury, providing exceptional service, gourmet meals, and well-appointed lodges.

- Amazonas Explorer

- Overview: Amazonas Explorer is a specialist in adventure travel in Peru, offering a range of activities from trekking to white-water rafting.
- Specialties: Trekking, mountain biking, and rafting.
- Popular Tours: Ultimate Inca Trail, Sacred Valley mountain biking, and Apurímac River rafting.
- Sustainability: Focuses on eco-friendly practices and works closely with local communities.

- Alpaca Expeditions

- Overview: Alpaca Expeditions is a locally-owned tour operator known for its exceptional service and personalized tours.
- Specialties: Hiking and trekking tours, including lesser-known trails.
- Popular Tours: Inca Trail, Salkantay Trek, and Choquequirao Trek.
- Unique Features: Emphasis on supporting local communities and providing high-quality gear and equipment for treks.

- Explorandes

- Overview: Explorandes has been a pioneer in adventure travel in Peru since 1975, offering a variety of outdoor activities.
- Specialties: Trekking, kayaking, and cultural tours.
- Popular Tours: Classic Inca Trail, Ausangate Trek, and multi-sport adventures in the Sacred Valley.
- Sustainability: Known for its commitment to sustainable tourism and environmental stewardship.

- Peru Eco Expeditions

- Overview: Peru Eco Expeditions offers customized eco-friendly tours that showcase Peru's natural beauty and cultural heritage.
- Specialties: Tailor-made itineraries, luxury eco-tours, and wildlife expeditions.
- Popular Tours: Custom adventures in the Amazon, luxury treks to Machu Picchu, and bespoke cultural tours.
- Sustainability: Focuses on minimizing environmental impact and supporting conservation initiatives.

- **Valencia Travel Cusco**

- Overview: Valencia Travel Cusco is a well-established tour operator offering a range of adventure and cultural tours in Peru.
- Specialties: Trekking, cultural tours, and multi-day adventures.
- Popular Tours: Inca Trail to Machu Picchu, Lares Trek, and Rainbow Mountain Tour.
- Unique Features: Personalized service, experienced guides, and a strong emphasis on cultural experiences.

- **Llama Path**

- Overview: Llama Path is a locally-owned tour operator known for its dedication to quality and sustainability.
- Specialties: Hiking and trekking tours.
- Popular Tours: Classic Inca Trail, Salkantay Trek, and the Choquequirao Trek.
- Sustainability: Committed to responsible tourism practices and supporting local communities.

These adventure tour operators provide a range of options for exploring Peru's diverse landscapes and rich cultural heritage. Whether you're trekking to Machu Picchu, navigating the Amazon, or surfing along the coast, these operators ensure a safe, enjoyable, and unforgettable experience.

Chapter 9: Practical Information

Currency and Money Exchange

Navigating currency and money exchange in a foreign country can be a crucial part of travel planning. Here's what you need to know about managing your finances while visiting Peru:

- **Peruvian Currency**

- Currency Name: The official currency of Peru is the Peruvian Sol, abbreviated as PEN. The symbol for the Sol is S/.
- Coins: The Peruvian Sol is subdivided into 100 céntimos. Coins are available in denominations of 1, 5, 10, 20, and 50 céntimos, as well as 1, 2, and 5 soles.
- Banknotes: Banknotes come in denominations of 10, 20, 50, 100, and 200 soles.

- **Exchange Rates**

- Exchange Rate: The exchange rate can fluctuate, so it's essential to check the current rate before

exchanging money. As of [Date], 1 USD is approximately [current exchange rate] PEN.
- Online Tools: Use reliable currency conversion websites or mobile apps to get real-time exchange rates.

- Where to Exchange Money

1. Banks:
   - Overview: Banks usually offer favorable exchange rates and are a reliable place to exchange money.
   - Tips: Carry your passport, as it may be required for transactions. Bank hours are typically Monday to Friday, 9 AM to 5 PM, and some may be open on Saturdays until noon.

2. Currency Exchange Offices (Casas de Cambio):
   - Overview: These specialized currency exchange offices are widely available in cities and tourist areas.
   - Tips: Compare rates at a few different locations to get the best deal. Always count your money and ensure the correct amount before leaving the counter.

3. ATMs:

- Overview: ATMs are widely available in cities and towns, and most accept international cards (Visa, MasterCard).
   - Tips: Use ATMs located inside banks or shopping centers for added security. Be aware of potential withdrawal fees and exchange rates applied by your home bank.

4. Hotels:
   - Overview: Many hotels offer currency exchange services, but the rates may not be as favorable as banks or exchange offices.
   - Tips: This can be a convenient option if you need a small amount of cash quickly.

5. Airports:
   - Overview: Currency exchange kiosks are available at major airports, but they often have higher fees and less favorable rates.
   - Tips: Consider exchanging only a small amount at the airport and wait to exchange larger amounts at banks or exchange offices in the city.

- **Tips for Handling Money**

1. Carry Small Bills and Coins:
   - Overview: Smaller denominations are useful for everyday purchases, public transportation, and tips.

- Tips: Vendors and taxi drivers may not always have change for larger bills, so carrying small bills and coins is practical.

2. Credit and Debit Cards:
- Overview: Credit and debit cards are widely accepted in cities, hotels, restaurants, and larger stores.
- Tips: Inform your bank of your travel plans to avoid any issues with card usage. Also, be aware of foreign transaction fees.

3. Avoid Counterfeit Bills:
- Overview: Counterfeit money can be an issue in Peru.
- Tips: Familiarize yourself with the look and feel of authentic Peruvian Soles. When receiving change, especially in small shops or from street vendors, examine the bills carefully.

4. Tipping:
- Overview: Tipping is customary in Peru, particularly in restaurants, hotels, and for tour guides.
- Tips: A tip of 10% is typical in restaurants if it's not already included in the bill. For hotel staff and guides, a small tip is appreciated.

5. Safety:
- Overview: Keep your money and valuables secure, especially in crowded areas and tourist spots.
- Tips: Use a money belt or hidden pouch to carry cash and important documents. Avoid displaying large amounts of money in public.

By understanding the local currency and following these tips for money exchange, you can manage your finances effectively and enjoy a smooth and stress-free experience in Peru.

Safety and Health

Traveling to Peru can be an exciting and enriching experience. However, like any destination, it's important to be aware of safety and health considerations to ensure a smooth and enjoyable trip. Here are some key tips and recommendations:

> Safety Tips

1. General Safety:
- Stay Alert: Be aware of your surroundings, especially in crowded places like markets, public transportation, and tourist attractions.

- Avoid Flashing Valuables: Keep your valuables such as jewelry, cameras, and expensive gadgets out of sight to avoid attracting unwanted attention.
- Secure Your Belongings: Use a money belt or hidden pouch to carry cash, credit cards, and important documents. Keep your backpack or bag in front of you in crowded areas.
- Use Reputable Transport: Opt for registered taxis or ride-hailing services like Uber. Avoid hailing taxis off the street, especially at night.
- Travel Insurance: Ensure you have comprehensive travel insurance that covers medical emergencies, trip cancellations, and theft or loss of belongings.

2. Pickpocketing and Scams:
- Be Cautious: Pickpocketing can occur in busy tourist areas. Keep your belongings secure and avoid carrying large amounts of cash.
- Avoid Scams: Be wary of common scams, such as someone "accidentally" spilling something on you and then offering to clean it up. Politely decline unsolicited offers of help or tours.

3. Health Precautions:
- Vaccinations: Make sure you are up to date with routine vaccinations. Additionally, consider

vaccinations for hepatitis A, typhoid, and yellow fever, especially if traveling to the Amazon region.

- Altitude Sickness: If traveling to high-altitude areas like Cusco or the Sacred Valley, acclimate gradually. Stay hydrated, avoid alcohol, and consider medication to prevent altitude sickness.

- Drink Bottled Water: Avoid drinking tap water. Stick to bottled water and ensure that ice in drinks is made from purified water.

- Food Safety: Enjoy the local cuisine but be cautious about street food. Eat at reputable restaurants and avoid raw or undercooked foods.

4. Natural Disasters:

- Earthquakes: Peru is prone to earthquakes. Familiarize yourself with safety procedures and know the emergency exits in your accommodation.

- Flooding and Landslides: During the rainy season (November to March), be aware of the potential for flooding and landslides, especially in mountainous regions.

Emergency Contacts

1. Emergency Numbers:
   - Police: 105
   - Fire Department: 116
   - Ambulance: 117

2. Embassy Contacts:
   - Carry the contact information of your country's embassy or consulate in Peru. They can assist in emergencies and provide support if needed.

3. Local Assistance:
   - Hospitals and Clinics: Know the location of nearby hospitals and clinics. In major cities, private hospitals generally offer higher standards of care.
   - Travel Insurance Hotline: Keep the emergency contact number for your travel insurance provider handy.

Health Tips

1. Altitude Sickness (Soroche):
   - Gradual Ascent: When traveling to high-altitude destinations, allow time to acclimate. Spend a couple of days in a lower altitude before heading to higher elevations.
   - Hydration: Drink plenty of water to stay hydrated. Herbal teas like coca tea can also help alleviate symptoms.
   - Medication: Consult with your doctor about medications like acetazolamide (Diamox) that can help prevent altitude sickness.

2. Water and Food Safety:
   - Bottled Water: Always drink bottled water and check that the seal is intact. Avoid ice unless

you are sure it's made from purified water.

- Food Hygiene: Choose restaurants with good hygiene practices. Opt for cooked foods and peel fruits before eating. Be cautious with street food.

3. Mosquito Protection:

- Insect Repellent: Use insect repellent with DEET, especially in the Amazon and other mosquito-prone areas.

- Protective Clothing: Wear long sleeves and pants, and sleep under mosquito nets if available.

- Preventive Measures: Consider antimalarial medication if traveling to high-risk areas. Consult a healthcare provider for recommendations.

4. Sun Protection:

- Sunscreen: Use a high-SPF sunscreen to protect against the strong Andean sun.

- Hat and Sunglasses: Wear a wide-brimmed hat and UV-protective sunglasses to shield against sun exposure.

5. Travel Health Kit:

- Essentials: Pack a basic travel health kit with items like pain relievers, antihistamines, anti-diarrheal medication, and a digital thermometer.

- Personal Prescriptions: Bring an adequate supply of any prescription medications you take regularly.

By following these safety and health tips, you can enjoy your travels in Peru with peace of mind and make the most of your adventure. Stay informed, be prepared, and take precautions to ensure a safe and healthy trip.

Transportation

Getting around Peru can be an exciting part of your travel adventure, with various transportation options available to suit different preferences and budgets. Here's a comprehensive guide to transportation in Peru:

Domestic Flights

1. Overview: Flying is the quickest way to cover long distances in Peru, especially between major cities and tourist destinations.
2. Airlines: LATAM, Avianca, Sky Airline, and Viva Air are some of the major domestic carriers.
3. Popular Routes: Lima to Cusco, Lima to Arequipa, Lima to Iquitos, and Cusco to Puerto Maldonado.
4. Tips: Book flights in advance to get the best rates. Check baggage allowances and arrive early at the airport, especially for flights to remote destinations.

Buses

1. Overview: Buses are the most common and economical way to travel across Peru. They offer varying levels of comfort and service.
2. Types:
    - Economy Buses: Basic services with frequent stops.
    - Mid-range Buses: More comfortable seats and fewer stops.
    - Luxury Buses: Reclining seats, onboard meals, and entertainment.
3. Popular Companies: Cruz del Sur, Oltursa, Movil Tours, and Civa.
4. Routes: Extensive network connecting cities, towns, and tourist sites.
5. Tips: For long-distance travel, opt for reputable companies and consider night buses with sleeper seats. Keep an eye on your belongings and use a money belt for valuables.

Trains

1. Overview: Trains are a scenic way to travel, especially to iconic destinations like Machu Picchu.
2. Routes:

- Cusco to Machu Picchu: Operated by PeruRail and Inca Rail, offering a range of service levels from budget to luxury.
- Cusco to Puno: The Andean Explorer, operated by PeruRail, provides a luxurious experience with stunning views of the Andes and Lake Titicaca.

3. Tips: Book train tickets well in advance, especially for popular routes to Machu Picchu. Choose your train class based on budget and comfort preferences.

Taxis and Ride-Hailing Services

1. Taxis:
   - Overview: Taxis are widely available in cities and towns.
   - Tips: Use registered or official taxis to ensure safety. Negotiate the fare before starting the journey, as most taxis do not have meters.

2. Ride-Hailing Services:
   - Overview: Uber, Cabify, and Beat are popular ride-hailing apps in major cities.
   - Tips: These services provide a convenient and often safer alternative to street taxis. Check the app for estimated fares and driver ratings.

Colectivos and Shared Vans

1. Overview: Colectivos are shared vans or minibusses that offer an affordable way to travel between cities and towns.
2. Routes: Commonly used for routes not well-served by regular buses.
3. Tips: They depart when full, so be prepared to wait. They can be crowded but are a cost-effective option for short distances.

Renting a Car

1. Overview: Renting a car offers flexibility for exploring Peru at your own pace.
2. Requirements: Valid driver's license, passport, and a credit card.
3. Tips: Consider renting a 4x4 for remote or rugged areas. Be aware of road conditions and local driving habits. Parking can be challenging in cities, so plan accordingly.

Boats and Ferries

1. Amazon River:
   - Overview: Riverboats and ferries are essential for travel in the Amazon region.
   - Routes: Popular routes include Iquitos to various Amazon lodges and towns.

- Tips: Choose reputable operators and be prepared for basic facilities on standard boats. Luxury cruises offer a more comfortable experience.
2. Lake Titicaca:
  - Overview: Boats and ferries connect Puno with islands like Uros, Taquile, and Amantani.
  - Tips: Guided tours often include boat transportation. Enjoy the scenic views and cultural experiences on the islands.

Bicycles and Motorbikes

1. Bicycles:
  - Overview: Renting a bicycle is a great way to explore cities and towns, especially in places like Lima, Cusco, and the Sacred Valley.
  - Tips: Use designated bike lanes where available and always wear a helmet.
2. Motorbikes:
  - Overview: Motorbikes can be rented in some tourist areas for more adventurous exploration.
  - Tips: Ensure you have the necessary driving experience and safety gear. Be cautious on busy roads.

Public Transportation

1. Buses:
   - Overview: City buses are an economical way to get around, but they can be crowded and routes may be confusing.
   - Tips: Ask locals or your accommodation for advice on bus routes and fares.
2. Metropolitan Areas:
   - Lima: The Metropolitano bus system and Line 1 of the Lima Metro provide efficient transportation in the capital.
   - Tips: Purchase a rechargeable card for the Metropolitano and plan your routes in advance.

By understanding the various transportation options available in Peru, you can choose the best modes of travel for your itinerary, ensuring a smooth and enjoyable journey. From the convenience of domestic flights to the scenic charm of train rides, Peru's diverse transportation network caters to all types of travelers.

Travel Tips

Traveling to Peru can be a wonderful adventure, filled with rich cultural experiences, stunning landscapes, and unique opportunities. To make the most of your trip, here are some essential travel tips that will help you navigate the country with ease and enjoyment:

> ➢ Planning and Preparation

1. Research and Plan Ahead:
   - Destinations: Identify the key destinations you want to visit, such as Lima, Cusco, Machu Picchu, the Sacred Valley, Lake Titicaca, and the Amazon Rainforest.
   - Itinerary: Create a flexible itinerary that allows for spontaneous discoveries. Include buffer days for rest and acclimatization, especially in high-altitude areas.

2. Travel Documents:
   - Passport: Ensure your passport is valid for at least six months beyond your travel dates.
   - Visas: Check if you need a visa to enter Peru. Many nationalities can enter visa-free for up to 90 days.
   - Copies: Make copies of your passport, visa, travel insurance, and important documents. Keep

one set with you and leave another with a trusted person back home.

3. Health Precautions:
   - Vaccinations: Consult your healthcare provider for recommended vaccinations, such as hepatitis A, typhoid, and yellow fever (especially for Amazon regions).
   - Medications: Carry a basic first-aid kit and any prescription medications you need. Consider bringing medication for altitude sickness if you plan to visit high-altitude areas.
   - Insurance: Purchase comprehensive travel insurance that covers medical emergencies, trip cancellations, and theft or loss of belongings.

> Packing Essentials

1. Clothing:
   - Layers: Pack clothing that can be layered to accommodate varying temperatures, especially in the Andes.
   - Comfortable Shoes: Bring sturdy, comfortable shoes for walking and hiking. Waterproof footwear is recommended for rainy regions.
   - Sun Protection: Include a wide-brimmed hat, sunglasses, and sunscreen with high SPF.

2. Travel Gear:
- Backpack: A daypack for daily excursions and a larger backpack or suitcase for your main luggage.
- Reusable Water Bottle: Stay hydrated and reduce plastic waste by carrying a reusable water bottle.
- Power Adapter: Peru uses Type A and Type C electrical outlets. Bring a suitable power adapter for your electronic devices.

3. Essential Items:
- Travel Guidebook: A good guidebook can provide valuable information and insights.
- Portable Charger: Keep your devices charged while on the go.
- Snacks: Pack some energy bars or snacks for long journeys.

➤ Cultural Tips

1. Learn Basic Spanish:
- Phrases: Learn some basic Spanish phrases to help with communication. Phrases like "Hola" (Hello), "Gracias" (Thank you), and "¿Dónde está el baño?" (Where is the bathroom?) can go a long way.
- Apps: Language translation apps can be helpful for more complex conversations.

2. Respect Local Customs:
  - Greetings: Greet people with a handshake or a kiss on the cheek, depending on the context.
  - Politeness: Use "por favor" (please) and "gracias" (thank you) in your interactions.
  - Dress Modestly: Especially when visiting religious sites or indigenous communities.

3. Cultural Sensitivity:
  - Photography: Always ask for permission before taking photos of people, especially in indigenous communities.
  - Tipping: Tipping is customary in restaurants, hotels, and for tour guides. A 10% tip is typical in restaurants.

  ➢ Staying Safe

1. Personal Safety:
  - Stay Vigilant: Be aware of your surroundings, especially in crowded areas and tourist hotspots.
  - Sccure Belongings: Use a money belt or hidden pouch for valuables and important documents.
  - Reputable Transport: Use registered taxis or ride-hailing services, and avoid hailing taxis off the street, especially at night.

2. Health and Hygiene:

- Drink Bottled Water: Avoid tap water and ice made from tap water. Drink bottled water or use a water purification system.
- Food Safety: Enjoy the local cuisine but be cautious with street food. Choose reputable restaurants and avoid raw or undercooked foods.

3. Natural Disasters:
- Earthquakes: Familiarize yourself with earthquake safety procedures. Know the emergency exits in your accommodation.
- Weather: Be prepared for varying weather conditions, especially if traveling during the rainy season (November to March).

➢ Transportation

1. Domestic Travel:
- Flights: Book domestic flights in advance for the best rates. Popular routes include Lima to Cusco and Lima to Iquitos.
- Buses: Opt for reputable bus companies for long-distance travel. Night buses with sleeper seats can save time and accommodation costs.

2. Local Transport:
- Taxis and Ride-Hailing: Use registered taxis or apps like Uber for convenience and safety.

- Public Transport: City buses and colectivos (shared vans) are economical options but can be crowded. Ask locals for guidance on routes.

3. Adventure Activities:
- Guided Tours: For activities like hiking, trekking, and wildlife tours, choose reputable tour operators with good reviews.
- Equipment: Ensure you have the right gear for your chosen activities, such as sturdy hiking boots and appropriate clothing.

By following these travel tips, you can make the most of your trip to Peru, ensuring a safe, enjoyable, and memorable experience. Embrace the adventure, immerse yourself in the rich culture, and explore the stunning landscapes that Peru has to offer.

Chapter 10: Conclusion

Summarizing the Journey

Peru is a country of immense natural beauty, rich cultural heritage, and endless opportunities for adventure. Our journey through the pages of this guide has taken us from the bustling streets of Lima to the ancient ruins of Machu Picchu, through the serene landscapes of the Sacred Valley, and into the depths of the Amazon Rainforest. Let's take a moment to reflect on the incredible experiences and insights we've gathered along the way:

➢ Exploring the Vibrant Cities

- Lima: Peru's capital, where history meets modernity, offers a taste of world-class cuisine, vibrant neighborhoods, and rich cultural experiences. From the historic center to the trendy district of Miraflores, Lima is a city that never ceases to captivate.
- Cusco: The former capital of the Inca Empire, Cusco is a city that blends ancient traditions with contemporary life. Its cobbled streets, Incan ruins, and bustling markets provide a unique glimpse into Peru's past and present.

- Arequipa: Known as the "White City" for its beautiful sillar stone architecture, Arequipa is a gem in the Peruvian Andes. Its colonial charm, stunning landscapes, and vibrant culinary scene make it a must-visit destination.

> ➤ **Discovering Natural Wonders**

- Machu Picchu: The crown jewel of Peru, this ancient Incan citadel stands as a testament to the ingenuity and resilience of the Inca civilization. Whether accessed via the iconic Inca Trail or a scenic train ride, Machu Picchu is a place of awe-inspiring beauty.
- Sacred Valley: A lush and fertile region dotted with traditional villages, Inca ruins, and breathtaking landscapes. The Sacred Valley offers a serene escape and an opportunity to connect with the Andean way of life.
- Amazon Rainforest: A journey into the Amazon is an immersion into one of the most biodiverse regions on Earth. From the bustling city of Iquitos to the remote lodges of Tambopata and Manu, the Amazon offers unparalleled wildlife encounters and jungle adventures.

> ➤ **Embracing Culture and Tradition**

- Festivals and Celebrations: Peru's vibrant festivals, such as Inti Raymi and Virgen de la Candelaria, showcase the country's rich cultural tapestry. These celebrations are a window into the traditions, music, dance, and spiritual beliefs of the Peruvian people.
- Local Cuisine: Peruvian cuisine is a delightful fusion of flavors, influenced by indigenous ingredients and diverse cultural influences. From the zesty ceviche to the hearty lomo saltado, the culinary journey in Peru is one of endless discovery.

> Adventure and Outdoor Activities

- Hiking and Trekking: Peru's diverse landscapes provide a playground for hikers and trekkers. Whether conquering the challenging Inca Trail, exploring the remote Ausangate Trek, or discovering the dramatic Colca Canyon, the opportunities for adventure are boundless.
- Wildlife and Nature Tours: From birdwatching in the Amazon to spotting condors in the Andes, Peru offers rich experiences for nature lovers. Guided tours and eco-lodges provide a deeper understanding of the country's unique ecosystems.
- Outdoor Sports: For thrill-seekers, Peru offers a range of outdoor activities, including mountain biking, surfing, white-water rafting, and

paragliding. The diverse terrain ensures there's something for every adventurer.

➢ **Practical Information**

- Safety and Health: With practical tips on staying safe and healthy, travelers can navigate Peru with confidence. From understanding local customs to being prepared for altitude sickness, careful planning ensures a smooth journey.
- Transportation: Efficient transportation options, including domestic flights, buses, trains, and taxis, make traveling across Peru convenient. Knowing the best ways to get around enhances the overall travel experience.

Peru is a land of contrasts and wonders, where ancient history meets modern innovation, and breathtaking landscapes blend with vibrant cultures. Whether you're exploring bustling cities, trekking through the Andes, or immersing yourself in the Amazon, Peru promises an unforgettable adventure. Embrace the journey, savor the experiences, and let the magic of Peru leave an indelible mark on your heart.

APPENDIX

A. Packing Checklist

- *Essentials*:
  - Passport and copies
  - Travel insurance documents
  - Cash and credit cards
  - Tickets and reservations

- *Clothing*:
  - Layered clothing for varying temperatures
  - Comfortable walking shoes
  - Waterproof jacket
  - Sun protection (hat, sunglasses, sunscreen)

- *Health and Safety*:
  - First aid kit
  - Prescription medications
  - Insect repellent
  - Hand sanitizer

- *Travel Gear:*
  - Reusable water bottle
  - Power adapter
  - Portable charger

B. Useful Spanish Phrases

- *Basic Greetings:*
  - Hello: Hola
  - Good morning: Buenos días
  - Good afternoon: Buenas tardes
  - Good evening: Buenas noches

- *Common Phrases:*
  - Please: Por favor
  - Thank you: Gracias
  - Excuse me: Disculpe / Perdón
  - How much does it cost?: ¿Cuánto cuesta?
  - Where is the bathroom?: ¿Dónde está el baño?

- *Emergency Phrases*:
  - Help!: ¡Ayuda!
  - Call a doctor!: ¡Llama a un doctor!
  - Police: Policía

C. Emergency Contacts
- Police: 105
- Fire Department: 116
- Ambulance: 117
- Embassy Contacts: [Insert relevant embassy contact information]

D. Recommended Reading and Viewing
- Books:
  - "Turn Right at Machu Picchu" by Mark Adams
  - "The Motorcycle Diaries" by Ernesto "Che" Guevara
  - "Inca Kola: A Traveller's Tale of Peru" by Matthew Parris

- Movies:
  - "The Motorcycle Diaries" (2004)
  - "Fitzcarraldo" (1982)
  - "The Emperor's New Groove" (2000)

- Documentaries:
  - "Nature: The Andes: The Dragon's Back" (PBS)
  - "Paddington" (2014) – A delightful film featuring scenes in Peru

E. Local Etiquette and Customs
- Greetings: Shake hands or kiss on the cheek in social settings.
- Personal Space: Peruvians may stand closer than what you might be accustomed to.
- Tipping: Common in restaurants and for guides; typically around 10%.

F. Important Websites and Apps
- Travel Information:
  - Official Peru Tourism Website: www.peru.travel
  - TripAdvisor: www.tripadvisor.com

- Language Translation:
  - Google Translate: www.translate.google.com
  - Duolingo: www.duolingo.com

- Transportation:
  - Rome2Rio: www.rome2rio.com
  - Uber: Available in major cities

- Health and Safety:
  - Centers for Disease Control and Prevention (CDC): www.cdc.gov
  - World Health Organization (WHO): www.who.int

MAPS

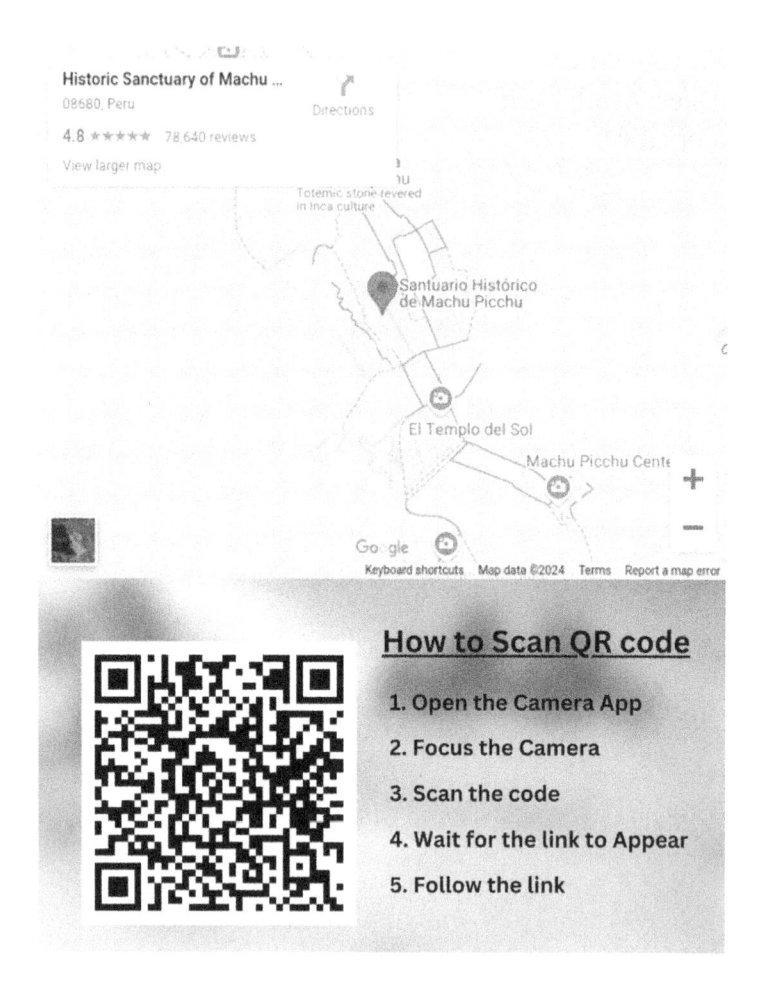

Historic Sanctuary of Machu ...
08680, Peru
4.8 ★★★★★ 78,640 reviews
View larger map

Totemic stone revered in Inca culture

Santuario Histórico de Machu Picchu

El Templo del Sol

Machu Picchu Cente

Google
Keyboard shortcuts   Map data ©2024   Terms   Report a map error

How to Scan QR code

1. Open the Camera App
2. Focus the Camera
3. Scan the code
4. Wait for the link to Appear
5. Follow the link

MACHU PICCHU

163

How to Scan QR code

1. Open the Camera App
2. Focus the Camera
3. Scan the code
4. Wait for the link to Appear
5. Follow the link

LIMA

How to Scan QR code

1. Open the Camera App
2. Focus the Camera
3. Scan the code
4. Wait for the link to Appear
5. Follow the link

CUSCO

Sacred Valley
08670, Peru

4.7 ★★★★★ 486 reviews

View larger map

Directions

Sacred Valley

Google
Keyboard shortcuts Map data ©2024 Terms Report a map error

How to Scan QR code

1. Open the Camera App
2. Focus the Camera
3. Scan the code
4. Wait for the link to Appear
5. Follow the link

SACRED VALLEY

Lake Titicaca

4.5 ★★★★★ 2,869 reviews

View larger map

Directions

MULTIVENTAS Y MULTISERVICIOS

Google
Keyboard shortcuts Map data ©2024 Terms Report a map error

How to Scan QR code

1. Open the Camera App
2. Focus the Camera
3. Scan the code
4. Wait for the link to Appear
5. Follow the link

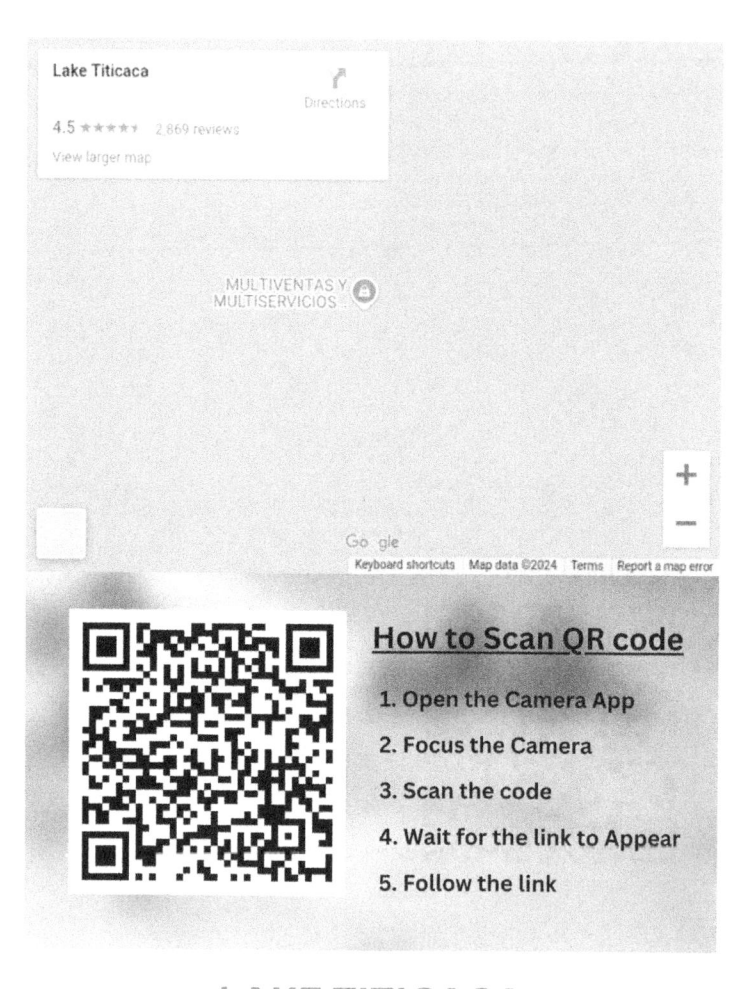

LAKE TITICACA

Reserva Nacional Tambopata
26 De Diciembre 270, Puerto Maldonado, Peru
4.7 ★★★★★ 575 reviews
View larger map

Reserva Nacional Tambopata

How to Scan QR code

1. Open the Camera App
2. Focus the Camera
3. Scan the code
4. Wait for the link to Appear
5. Follow the link

Amazon Rainforest (Tambopata National Reserve)

Made in United States
Orlando, FL
20 February 2025